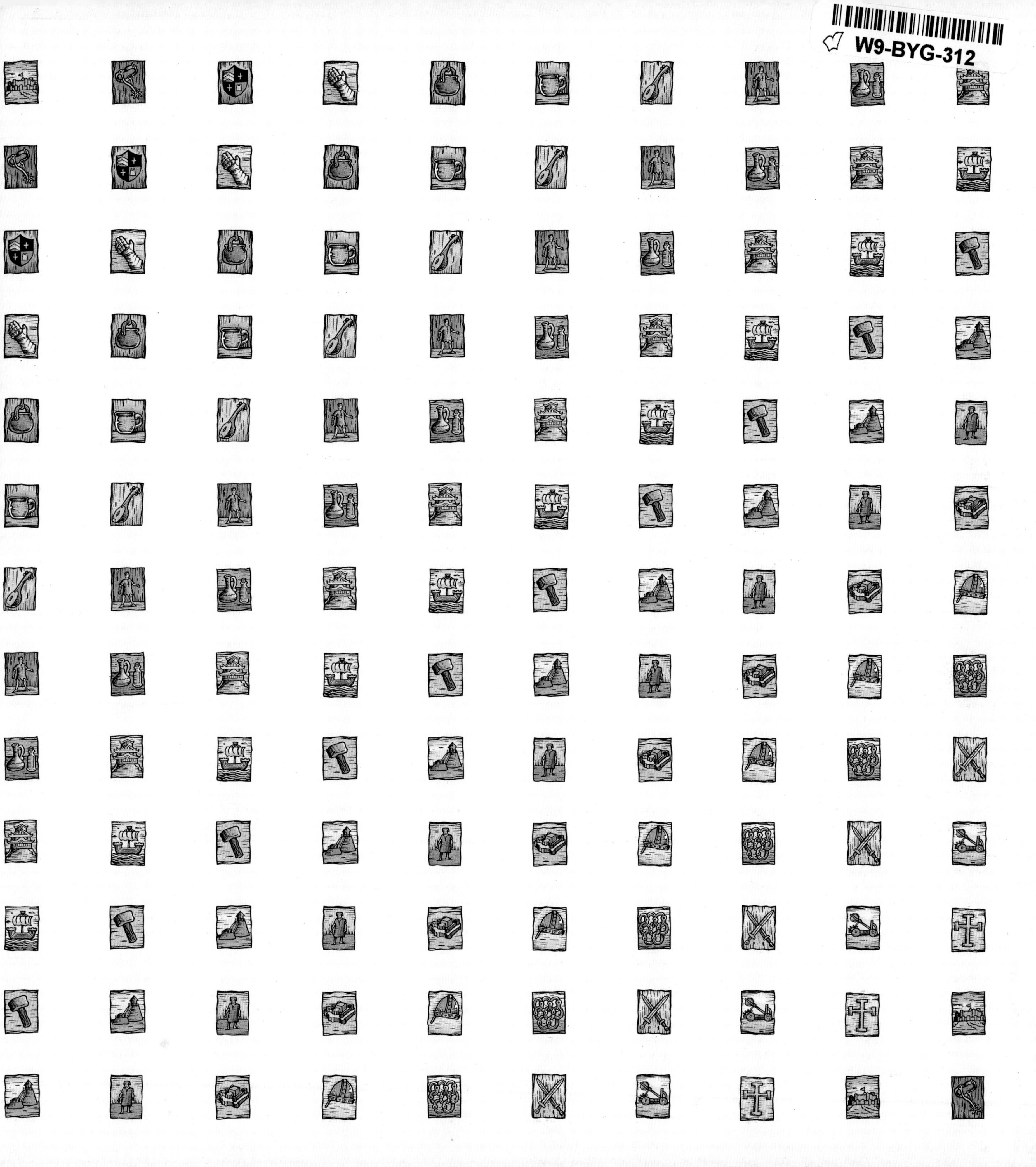

CASTLE

CASTLE

STRUAN REID

BARNES
&NOBLE
BOOKS
NEW YORK

A QUARTO CHILDREN'S BOOK

This edition published by Barnes & Noble, Inc.,
by arrangement with Quarto Children's Books

1996 Barnes & Noble Books

ISBN 0-7607-0214-4
M 10 9 8 7 6 5 4 3 2 1

CREATIVE DIRECTOR Louise Jervis
SENIOR ART EDITOR Nigel Bradley
PROJECT EDITOR Simon Beecroft
EDITOR John Kirkwood
VISUALISATION AND DESIGN Roger Hutchins
PAGE MAKE-UP Nik Morley
PICTURE MANAGERS Vicky King and Su Alexander
INDEXER Hilary Bird
CONSULTANT Elizabeth Hallam

ILLUSTRATORS
Julian Baker, Christian Hook, Roger Hutchins, and Roger Stewart

PICTURE CREDITS
a = *above*, b = *below*, c = *center*, r = *right*, l = *left*

Ace Photo Agency: *John Lambie* 44 / *Mike Lethby* 45*al* / *Mauritius* 45*r*
Bodleian Library: 1, 6*bl*, 8*a*, 20*ar*, 23*ar*, 28*br*, 29, 31*ar*, 35, 36*al*, 36*br*, 37, 40*al*, 40*bc*, 42
British Museum: 30 Peter Clayton: 13, 26 E.T. Archive: 3, 15*al*, 21*ar*, 22*al*,
28*a*, 31*al*, 31*br*, 33, 34, 36*bl*, 38, 40*br*, 43*l* Life File: *Richard Powers* 7*ar* /
Andrew Ward 8*b* / *Wayne Shakell* 11*a* The Mansell Collection: 6*bc*, 12*a*, 25*br*, 28*bl*
Mike Sharp Photography: 6*al*, 12*b*, 15*ar* The Wellcome Institute Library: 43*r*

Library of Congress Cataloguing data available upon request

Manufactured by Bright Arts Pte, Singapore
Printed by Winner Offset Co, Hong Kong

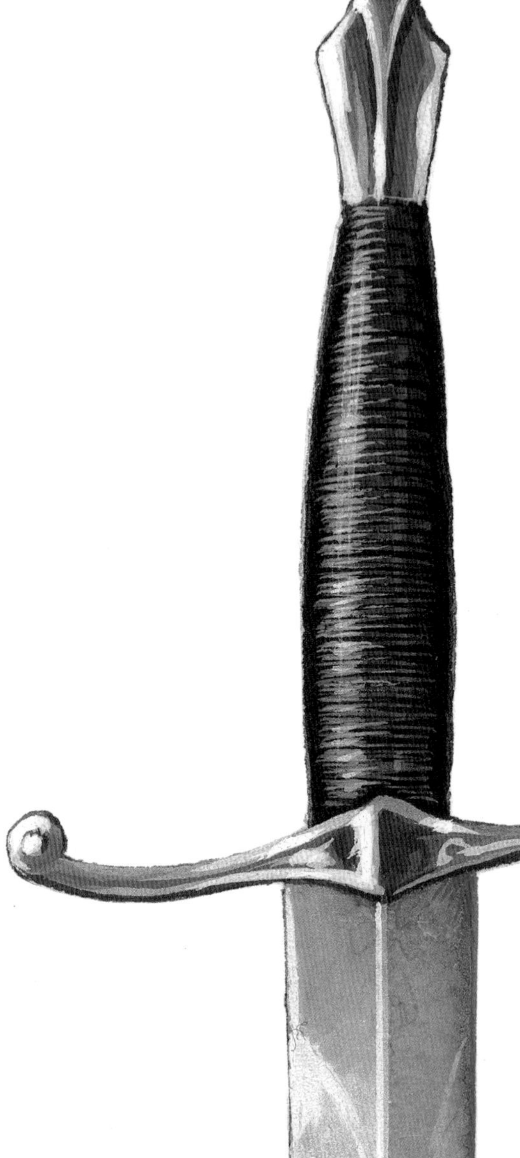

CONTENTS

Castle times

The medieval period, which lasted from about 500 A.D. to 1500 A.D., was a time of war. Life revolved around castles, great strongholds giving protection from enemy armies.

In the central and later Middle Ages, from about 1000 A.D. to 1500 A.D., many of the castles we can see today were built. Thousands were constructed throughout Europe and the Middle East, from the misty expanses of Ireland in the west to the mountains and deserts of Syria and Jordan in the east.

Castles were great strongholds that controlled vast areas of land, often farther than the eye could see. The thick, robust castle walls provided protection from attacking armies. From the battlements, the defenders showered the heads of the attackers with deadly weapons.

Within the castle walls

In times of trouble, many people who lived in the countryside found

▲ *In the Middle Ages, kings made all the laws. They were protected by lords and knights.*

▼ *Most peasants worked in the fields. Others, such as blacksmiths, potters, and millers, practiced a craft.*

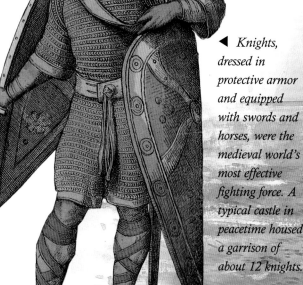

◀ *Knights, dressed in protective armor and equipped with swords and horses, were the medieval world's most effective fighting force. A typical castle in peacetime housed a garrison of about 12 knights.*

Standing guard

Castles were designed to guard and protect strategic areas such as coastlines, mountain passes, valleys, or river estuaries.

protection within the castle walls. But castles also served as homes for kings, princes, or great lords and their families. Here, they lived and entertained friends and visitors. Many servants helped in the smooth running of the castle, and there were often so many people living in it that it looked like a small town, with living quarters, workshops, stables, wells, and barns for storing food.

FIGHTING FOR A HOLY CAUSE

By 700 A.D., the land of Palestine in the Middle East, where Jesus lived and died, were ruled by Muslims. At the end of the 11th century, the Christian Church launched a number of military campaigns, called Crusades, to take them back. Thousands of Christian soldiers set out for the Middle East. They became known as Crusaders.

As the Crusaders captured lands in the Middle East, they built castles to provide themselves with more permanent bases.

By the time of the last Crusade in the 13th century, however, all of Palestine had been recaptured by the Muslims.

◀ *A Muslim soldier prepares for battle in this medieval picture.*

▲ *Castles in the Middle East, such as this one in Syria, were attacked by Crusaders.*

SOCIETY AT WORK

Medieval society was organized by ranks. People were clear about their status. The king, at the top, was usually the most powerful person because he had the support of the Church and owned the most land. He granted some of this land to nobles called barons who, in return, promised to fight for him. They in turn granted part of their land to their supporters, including knights. This system is called feudalism.

Village stores
Villages supplied the castle with food. In times of trouble, the villagers found refuge within the castle walls.

Working in the fields
At the bottom of "feudal" society were the peasants who worked on the lord's land in return for his protection.

Hilltop fortresses
Castles were built in commanding positions overlooking the surrounding countryside.

Master of all he sees
Lords lived in castles and controlled one or more "manors," typically consisting of a village or villages, a church, fields, and forests.

Building the castle

Castle construction was a tremendous operation. Hundreds of workers – some skilled, some not – worked under the command of a master mason.

Once a site had been chosen for a new castle, usually one dominating the surrounding land and with a supply of fresh water, the king or baron asked the master mason to plan and build it. The operation could take as long as 10 or even 20 years, and the work involved an enormous amount of organization.

After about 1100, castles were usually built of stone rather than wood – which was easily set on fire by attacking armies– so expert stonemasons had to be hired. Among other workers needed were carpenters who cut wooden beams and made doors and shutters. Blacksmiths provided ironwork and hinges, and made, sharpened, and mended tools. The master mason's design was marked out on the ground with ropes and stakes. The walls – some of which were 16 feet (5 m) thick at the base – were built on deep foundations. Battlements were finished last.

CASTLE IN KENT

The 14th-century castle of Bodiam in Kent, England, was built to repel French pirate marauders of the Channel ports. The castle, which has a wide moat, was designed so all of the curtain walls (walls between towers) could be defended by weapons fired from its towers.

◀ *Bodiam was built when gunpowder was becoming a threat. It has gunports in its walls.*

WORKERS IN STONE

Up to 1,000 workers might be used to build a castle. During the construction of Harlech Castle, in Wales, for instance, records from 1286 show a typical weekly labor force of 520 unskilled workers, 170 masons, 90 quarry workers, 28 carpenters, 26 administrative staff, and 24 blacksmiths. Workers were often forced into service so some sites were guarded to stop desertion.

Building material

Blacksmith

Temporary camp Workers lived inside stockades during the building season, which lasted from April to November.

◀ *A castle construction site had many different craftsmen working on it. As walls rose higher, wooden scaffolding went up. Masons cut and fashioned stone into blocks of the desired shape. These blocks were raised to the top with ropes and pulleys.*

Stony exterior
Inner and outer wall faces were stone. In the gap between were mortar, rubble, and flints for strength.

Lifting stones
Large blocks were lifted by a wooden crane operated by a man walking around inside a giant wheel.

Assembling material
If large stones were not locally available, theys had to be brought from quarries by land, using wagons or pack horses, or by river, and sometimes by sea.

A tour of the castle

From what is left of castles today, it is possible to figure out what they were like when they were bustling with life and had a vital role to play.

Many castles survive – some nearly complete, some in ruins. The huge walls – once patrolled by watchful soldiers – are often still standing to quite a height, sometimes encircled by a deep defensive ditch, the moat. On the walls of the main entrance, or gatehouse, might be seen holes that were the hanging points for the castle's great wood and iron doors.

Inside the castle

The most massive remains of the castle are probably its keep, or donjon, the biggest and strongest part of the building. Walking around inside, you might be able to see the remains of the Great Hall with its huge arches, delicately

▼ *Ancestors of the medieval castle were Iron Age hill forts or fortified towns. These were surrounded by ditches and ramparts and had wooden walls.*

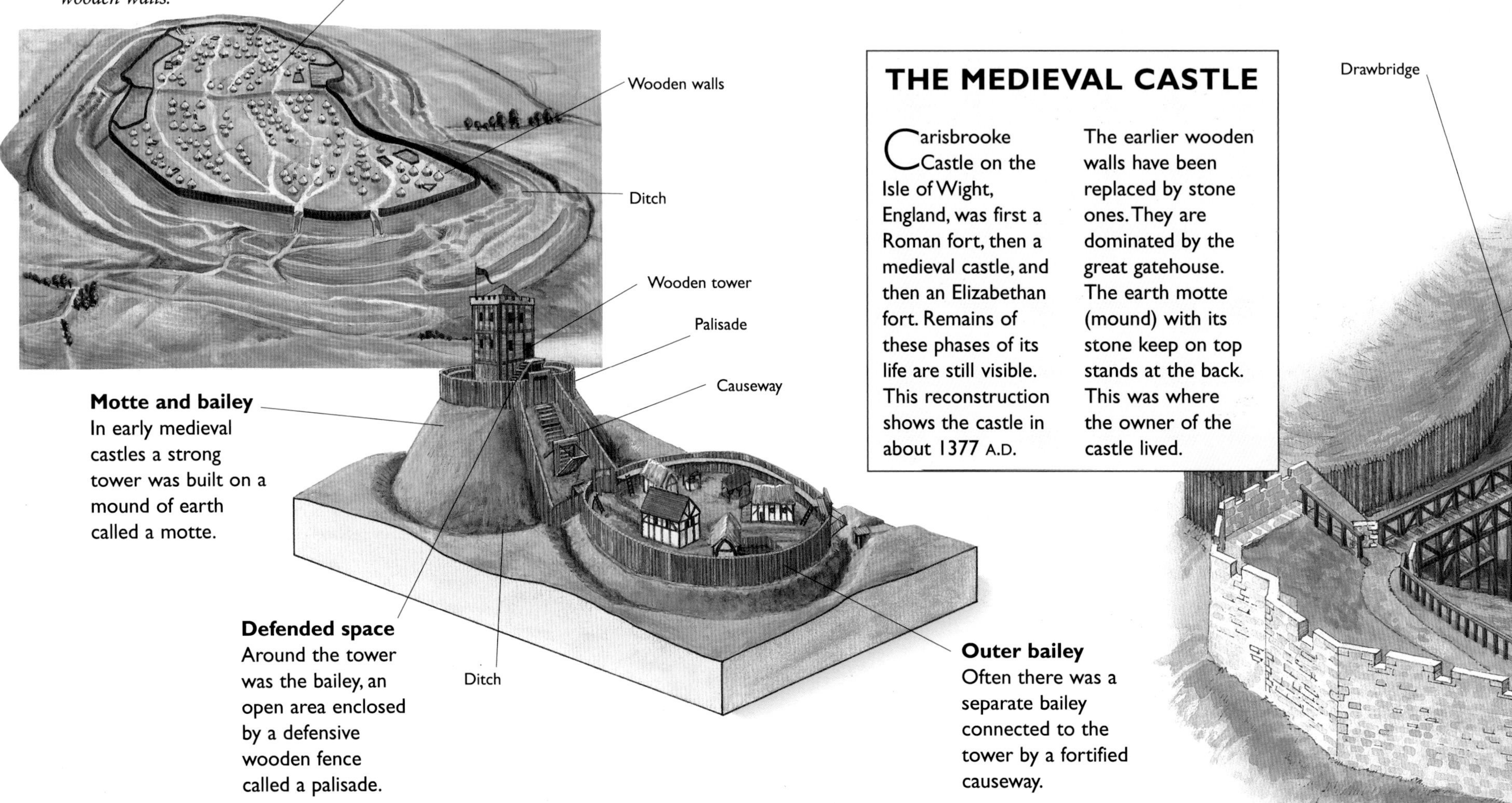

Motte and bailey
In early medieval castles a strong tower was built on a mound of earth called a motte.

Defended space
Around the tower was the bailey, an open area enclosed by a defensive wooden fence called a palisade.

Outer bailey
Often there was a separate bailey connected to the tower by a fortified causeway.

THE MEDIEVAL CASTLE

Carisbrooke Castle on the Isle of Wight, England, was first a Roman fort, then a medieval castle, and then an Elizabethan fort. Remains of these phases of its life are still visible. This reconstruction shows the castle in about 1377 A.D.

The earlier wooden walls have been replaced by stone ones. They are dominated by the great gatehouse. The earth motte (mound) with its stone keep on top stands at the back. This was where the owner of the castle lived.

carved windows, and enormous fireplaces where lords and ladies warmed themselves in the cold of winter. Nearby is the chapel and at the bottom of the towers, there are doors to spiral staircases which corkscrew their way up to the battlements above. If you climb to the top, you can see far into the distance over the surrounding country, like the lookouts of old.

▶ *Harlech Castle in Wales has a central fortress ringed by low outer walls. These walls were further protected by weapons fired from inner walls.*

The castle community

A castle was the focal point for those who lived nearby. It was a center for trade and a refuge in times of trouble.

▼ *Churches were a focal point within the castle for those living in or dependent on the castle. Often the castle's lord is remembered in a stained glass window, dressed in his finery but in a humble posture nevertheless.*

In medieval times, most people did not live in towns, but in small villages and isolated hamlets in the countryside. From dawn until dusk the peasants spent most of their time in the large open fields surrounding their houses.

The people in the castle and town depended upon the country people to supply them with food and the raw materials they needed for their trades and craft. Peasants traveled to the towns with grain, animals, fresh fruit, and vegetables. They also brought wool and leather for making clothes and shoes. But when danger threatened, the peasants depended on the castle, and they would seek safety behind its fortified walls.

After a castle had been built, a town would sometimes grow up, with small houses and businesses clusteried around its walls. The king

CASTLE-TOWNS

Where whole towns were enclosed by fortifications, people lived in tall narrow houses, crowded together over and around shops and workshops. These castle-towns were very busy and exciting places to live. Examples of castle-towns include Caernarfon in Wales and Kerak in Jordan. The towns usually grew so much over the years that they extended well beyond the original walls.

Market fun
Traveling musicians, jugglers, and actors came to entertain the people. Stands sold food and drink.

Church

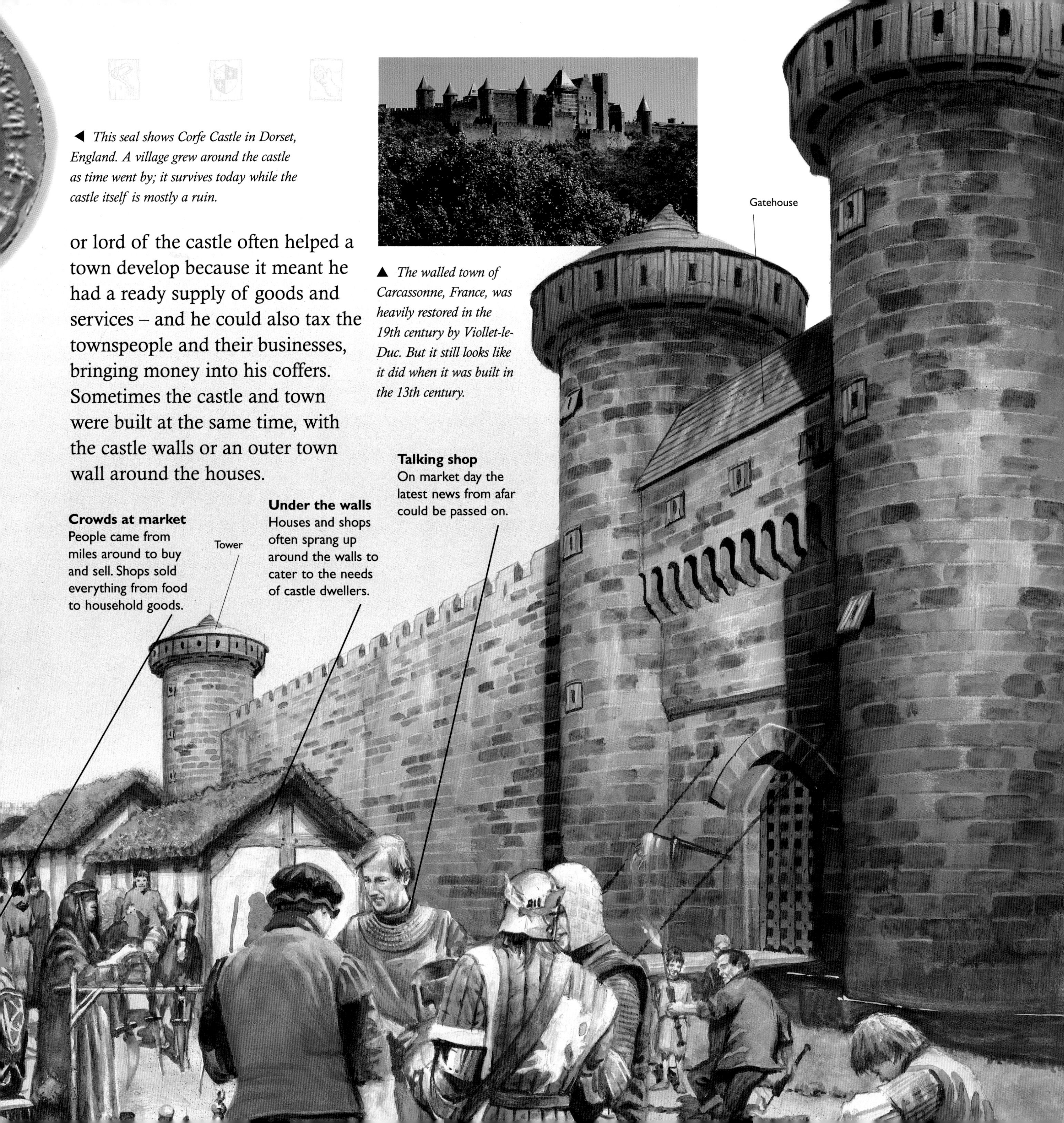

◀ *This seal shows Corfe Castle in Dorset, England. A village grew around the castle as time went by; it survives today while the castle itself is mostly a ruin.*

▲ *The walled town of Carcassonne, France, was heavily restored in the 19th century by Viollet-le-Duc. But it still looks like it did when it was built in the 13th century.*

or lord of the castle often helped a town develop because it meant he had a ready supply of goods and services – and he could also tax the townspeople and their businesses, bringing money into his coffers. Sometimes the castle and town were built at the same time, with the castle walls or an outer town wall around the houses.

Crowds at market
People came from miles around to buy and sell. Shops sold everything from food to household goods.

Under the walls
Houses and shops often sprang up around the walls to cater to the needs of castle dwellers.

Talking shop
On market day the latest news from afar could be passed on.

A center of defense

A well-designed castle presented a series of difficult challenges to any force that might try to attack it.

Attacking armies would be confronted with a huge ditch called a moat that surrounded the castle. This was designed to prevent attackers from getting right up to the walls. It was sometimes filled with water, but was often left dry and filled with pointed wooden stakes.

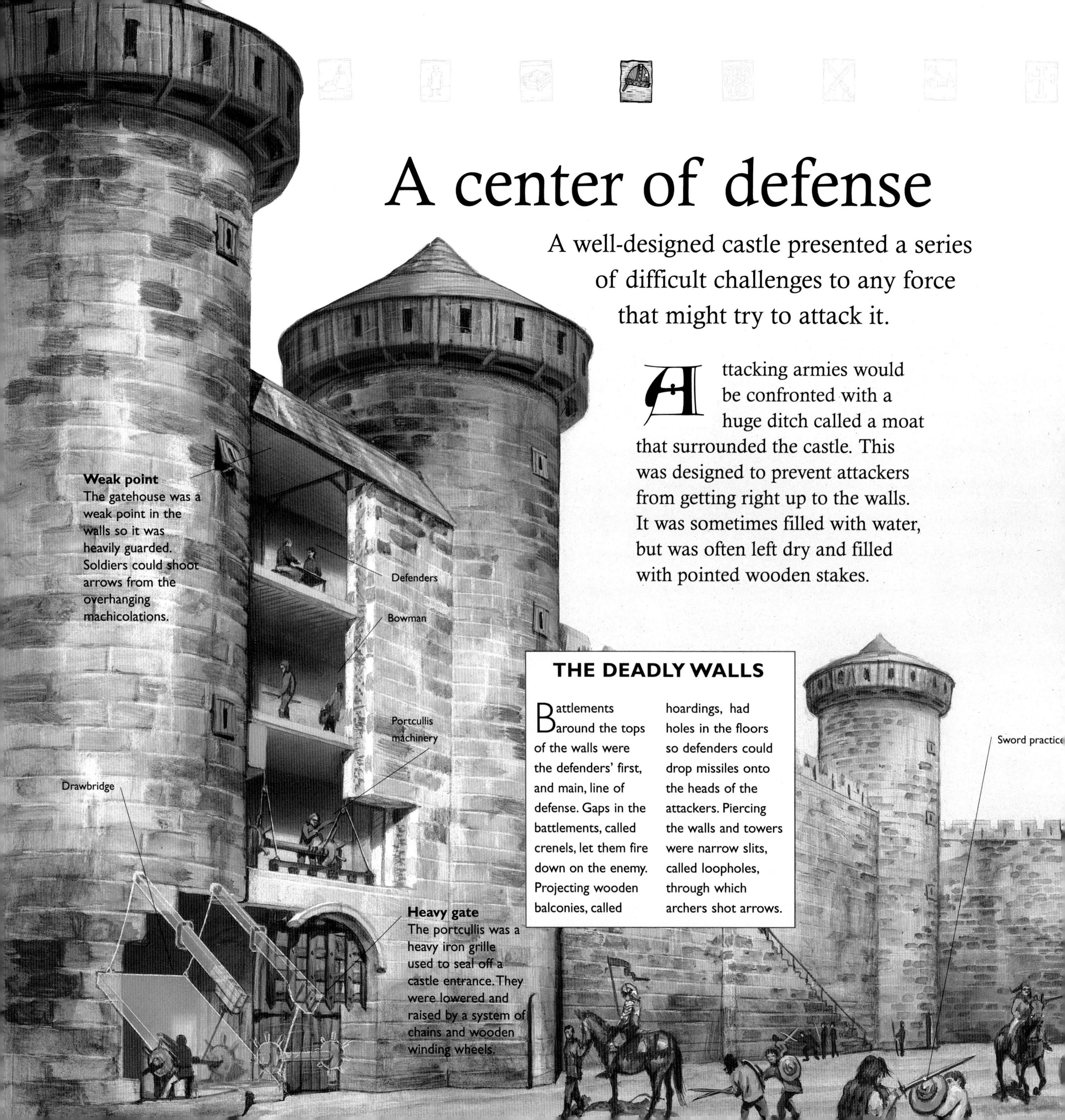

Weak point
The gatehouse was a weak point in the walls so it was heavily guarded. Soldiers could shoot arrows from the overhanging machicolations.
Defenders
Bowman
Portcullis machinery
Drawbridge
Heavy gate
The portcullis was a heavy iron grille used to seal off a castle entrance. They were lowered and raised by a system of chains and wooden winding wheels.
Sword practice

THE DEADLY WALLS

Battlements around the tops of the walls were the defenders' first, and main, line of defense. Gaps in the battlements, called crenels, let them fire down on the enemy. Projecting wooden balconies, called hoardings, had holes in the floors so defenders could drop missiles onto the heads of the attackers. Piercing the walls and towers were narrow slits, called loopholes, through which archers shot arrows.

▶ *It was the increasing use of weapons such as cannons that eventually made castles unnecessary.*

A drawbridge over the moat could be pulled up by chains. There was a thick wood and iron door which could be locked and bolted with iron bars. A heavy iron grille called the portcullis could be dropped in front of the door. If they reached the walls, the enemy was confronted with the main defenses, the walls themselves, and the deadly fire from the defenders on the battlements and towers.

GUARDING THE GATE

Harlech Castle in Wales was built in the later part of the 13th century. It was one of the so-called concentric design of castle because it had layers of defenses one inside the other. This design did not have a keep as such. The outer gatehouse has two massive outer defensive towers for protection. Beyond the main gatehouse was an inner keep-gatehouse (shown above right).

On guard
Even in peacetime, soldiers kept a lookout on the walls. An unguarded castle could easily be taken in a surprise attack.

Last resort
The keep was the castle's strongest part. Defenders went there if the rest of the castle was overrun.

Fighting twist
Spiral staircases often twisted clockwise so attacking soldiers coming up were at a disadvantage with little room to wield a sword in the right hand.

Ready to fight
The castle's garrison practiced their fighting skills regularly to be ready to defend their castle.

Defenders of the castle

The soldiers who lived in the castle and acted as its fighting force were called the garrison.

In times of peace, there was usually only a small garrison, but in war the numbers were swelled by soldiers who came to defend their lord and his lands. Even in these times of trouble, most castles had no more than about 100 soldiers in the garrison. The enormous crusader castle of Krak des Chevaliers in Syria (see pages 26–27) had more than 2,000, however.

A knight's duty

Early in the medieval period, a castle's garrison usually consisted of knights who were vassals – landholders who owed allegiance to

Ready for battle
The castle armorer always had to make sure that there were enough weapons – including longbows and arrows – available in the event of hostilities.

Arrows ready
Bowmen kept their arrows ready at their side, either stuck in the ground or laid out so they could shoot fast.

MURDER HOLES

Machicolations were stone walkways that hung over the tops of castle walls or towers. Openings in the floor allowed defenders to pour boiling water, hot sand, or heavy rocks down onto attackers. The defenders remained hidden behind protective stone walls. Many castles had similar holes, called *meutriers* or murder holes, in the gatehouse ceiling – a valuable defense if the enemy managed to get through the portcullis.

Defenders also poured water through these holes to put out fires.

the lord. These knights would take turns to do their garrison duty – once one knight came off duty and returned to his estates, he would be replaced by another. There were also paid knights, foot soldiers, and archers, the retinue of the lord, who were armed and ready for action.

STRAIGHT AIM

The name for places where archers went to practice their skill was the butts (from an Old French word meaning target). Accuracy with the bow was a highly valued skill.

Garrison members escorted the lord and his family as they went about their business outside the castle, protecting them from robbers and any marauding soldiers. They were armed with daggers, swords, longbows, and crossbows.

Fighting man
An armed man looks at the target while the archer shoots. Defenders would use swords only at close quarters if the attackers breached or scaled the walls.

Chain mail

Padded jerkin (a sleeveless and collarless jacket)

Swords were kept in holders called scabbards

Target

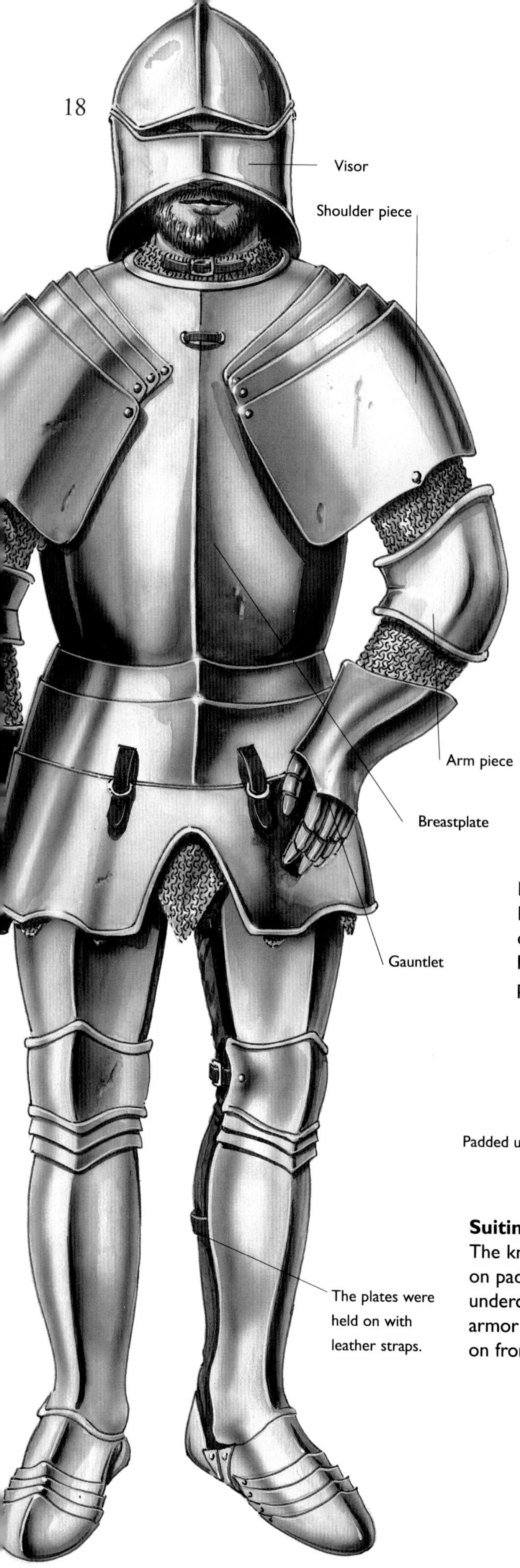

Visor
Shoulder piece
Arm piece
Breastplate
Gauntlet
The plates were held on with leather straps.

Armor

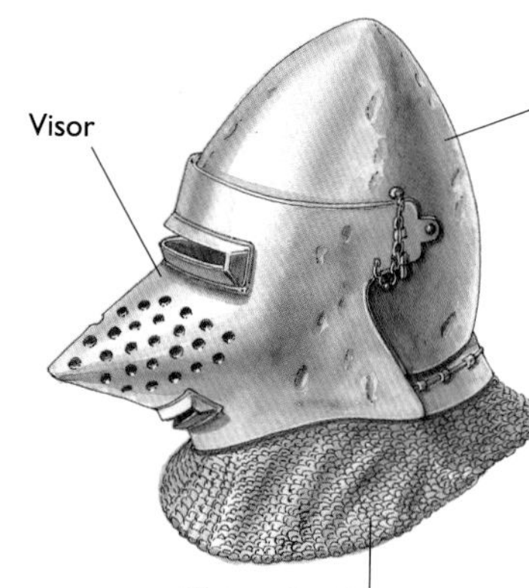

Covered from head to toe with steel armor, the knight struck fear into his foes. Mounted and armored, a knight was a mighty force.

Visor
Chainmail collar

The earliest type of armor was made of panels of thick leather stitched together. Then knights started to wear chainmail. This was a heavy but flexible type of armor made from hundreds of small iron rings linked together. Chainmail was worn over thick, padded underclothes which helped to absorb the blows from swords and other weapons. During the 1100s, knights started to cover more of their bodies with chainmail. They had sleeves, leggings, and even gloves of mail.

But chainmail was flexible, so a really powerful blow from a sword

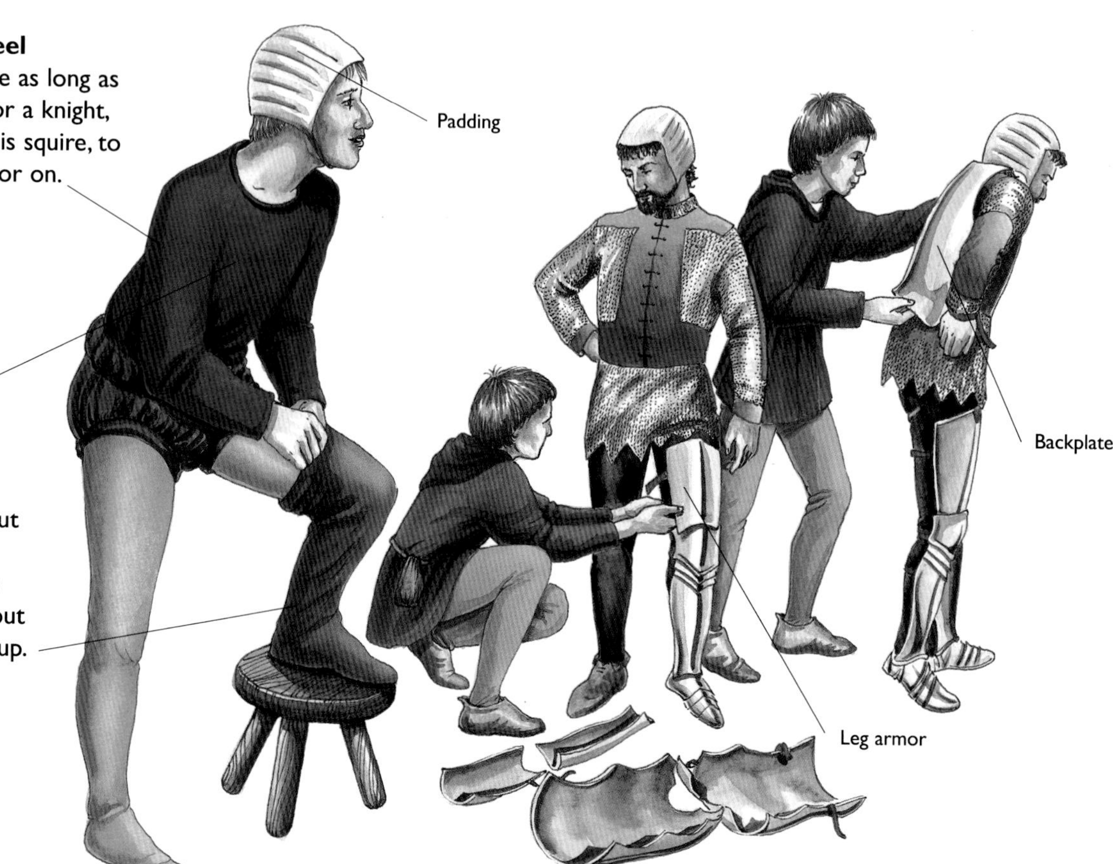

Man of steel
It could take as long as one hour for a knight, helped by his squire, to put his armor on.

Padding
Padded underclothes
Backplate
Leg armor

Suiting up
The knight first put on padded underclothes. The armor was then put on from the feet up.

Head protection
The knight's helmet, or *basinet*, had a visor, which could be lifted up, and was pierced with breathing holes. Around his neck was a chainmail collar.

could break bones, and the mail could be pierced by arrows. So knights started to add plates of steel armor to give extra protection, covering their knees, chests, thighs, and arms. Toward the end of the medieval period, knights were wearing complete suits of armor plating. They were jointed to allow movement.

Plate armor gave more protection than chainmail, but gaps between the plates could be pierced by pointed swords and plates could be pierced by short, powerful arrows called bolts fired by crossbows. The wearer could also get extremely hot beneath it all.

IN SHINING ARMOR

Knights and lords might wear elaborate suits of armor, made of colored and gilded (gold-plated) steel. Some were intricately engraved, while others were made to look like pleated material. These fantastic suits were worn in parades, for display, or in tournaments. Prince Edward, son of King Edward III of England, became known as the Black Prince because of the color of his jousting armor.

Shaffron
Crinet
Chain links
Horse coat

HORSE ARMOR

Sometimes the knight's horse was dressed in steel armor. A *shaffron* covered the head; the neck was protected by a jointed piece called a *crinet*. Underneath was a coat of chainmail. The armored knight and horse together acted like an armored tank. But horse armor was costly and worn only rarely.

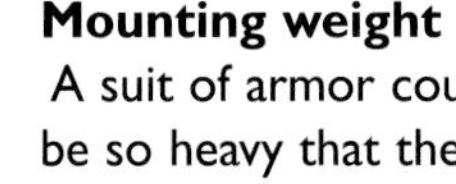

Mounting weight
A suit of armor could be so heavy that the knight had to be helped onto his horse by the squire.

Dressed to kill
Full armor could weigh as much as 70 pounds (32 kg). But the weight was evenly spread over the body, and the plates moved separately from each other so the knight was able to move around relatively easily in battle.

Weapons of war

Knights and the other soldiers in a medieval army had an array of deadly weapons at their disposal.

▲ *Richard I, the Lionheart, King of England, was a renowned warrior and as such would have been familiar with the weapons of his day. Here, he is shown fighting Saladin, the leader of the Muslim armies.*

▼ *The weapons used in medieval fighting were designed to cut, pierce, or stun. But a weapon is only as dangerous as the man wielding it, so soldiers drilled constantly to perfect their fighting skills.*

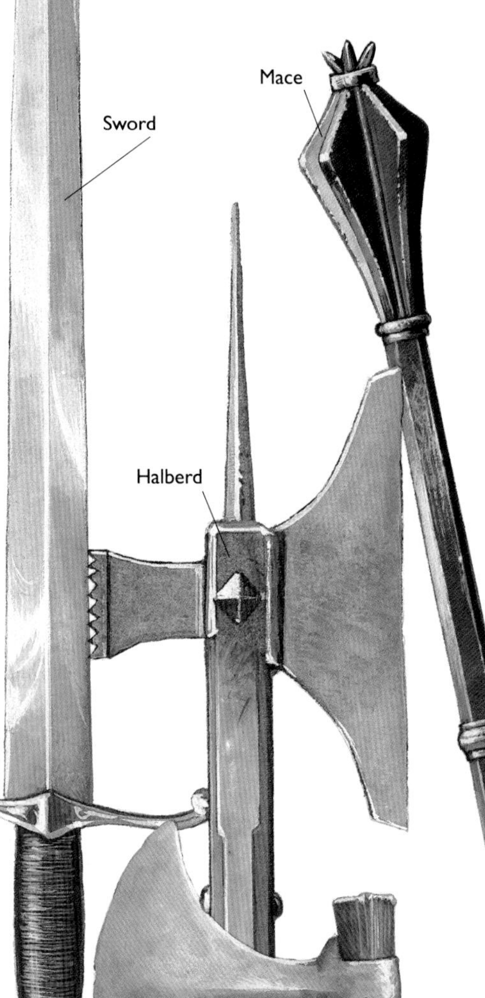

When they charged into battle on their horses, knights carried long lances which they lowered and used to try to knock an opponent knight off his horse. But the main weapon – used in the knighting ceremony itself – was a knight's sword. Well into the medieval period, knights used heavy doubled-edged swords which they swung around and slashed at their enemies, who wore coats of mail.

Tools of the deadly trade

In the 13th century, plate armor became more common and this gave better protection against these sharp blades. So swords with pointed ends were used to penetrate the thin gaps between the plates of armor. Knights and mounted soldiers might also carry daggers, short axes, and sticks with heavy weights on the end, called maces, which they used to club their opponents over the head and stun them. Shields were carried to deflect the enemy blows.

Hand to hand
Two soldiers fight to the death armed with halberds (fearsome blades attached to long poles).

Spoils of war
After a battle, the field was strewn with the dead. Their weapons were quickly collected by the winning army for reuse.

As the knights thundered into battle, they came under attack from lines of foot soldiers who stabbed at them and their horses with long spears. These soldiers also had short daggers and blades on long poles called halberds.

LONGBOW vs. CROSSBOW

In open warfare, the longbow was reckoned to be superior since its firing rate, 12 arrows a minute, was five times that of the crossbow. In sieges the more powerful crossbow were better.

▶ *English archers at the battle of Crecy, fought in 1346, took a heavy toll on the French army. They used thin but heavy armor-piercing arrowheads called bodkins.*

MAKING WEAPONS

The armorer had to make sure that there was a stockpile of weapons to cope with a long siege. Working with iron and steel, and hammering out components on an anvil, an armorer and his assistants could make anything from a suit of armor itself to a sword blade. In wartime he would constantly be repairing weapons and armor, and making new arrowheads and crossbow bolts.

Invulnerable?
A fully armed and armored knight was virtually invulnerable to all but another armed like him.

Out to fight
Knights on horseback would choose the best moment to leave the castle and attack the enemy.

Under siege

In times of war, castles came under attack. But how did enemy armies overpower these mighty defenses?

Castles were built for defense and were designed to repel enemy soldiers. But in times of war, they might come under siege, when attacking armies tried to prevent anyone from coming in or out of the castle. If it could not be taken quickly, by intimidation, trickery, or bribery, the enemy tried to starve the occupants into surrendering. If this did not work, they finally tried to take the enemy castle by force. By this time the defenders were usually weakened by hunger.

Castles were designed to hold out against a siege for as long as possible. There were wells and stashes of food to last the defenders until help came from another castle.

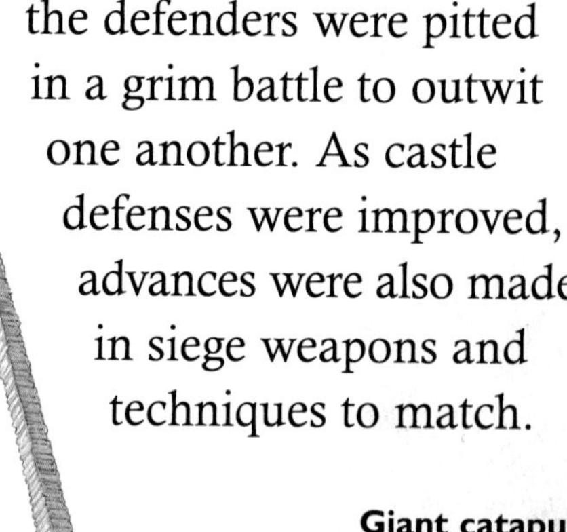

The attacking army and the defenders were pitted in a grim battle to outwit one another. As castle defenses were improved, advances were also made in siege weapons and techniques to match.

UNDERMINING THE WALLS

Sometimes the attackers dug a tunnel under the castle walls. The tunnel itself was supported with wooden beams that were burned as the soldiers left. This caused the tunnel to collapse, which would then bring part of the castle wall above crashing down.

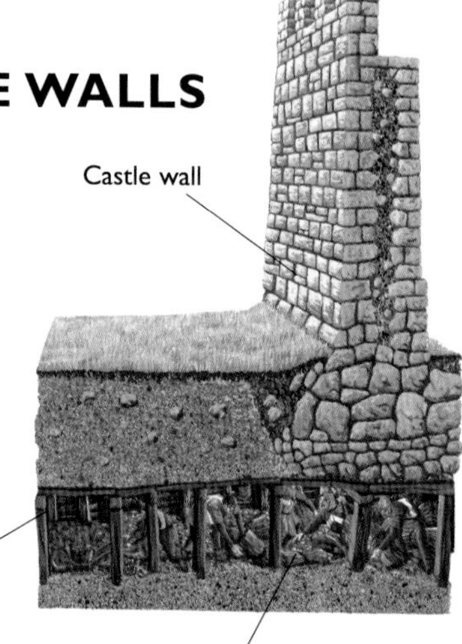

Giant catapult Trebuchets were used to batter enemy walls. Rocks, placed in a sling on one end, were propelled through the air by the use of a heavy counterweight.

Battles in the belfry Belfries were tall wooden towers on wheels that were pushed right up to the castle walls so attackers could jump over. Belfries were covered in animal hides to protect against fire.

Soldiers on scaling ladders
Battering the walls
Battering rams were pushed against the castle walls. Soldiers who worked them were protected from falling missiles by wooden casings.
Rain of arrows
The defenders shot arrows through slit-like windows and from over the castle's battlements.
Mighty mangonel
The mangonel was another kind of catapult. Its firing arm was pulled back by twisting a rope around a circular beam.

◀ *Besieging soldiers climb scaling ladders and hack at a castle's foundations in this medieval book illustration.*

◀ *Women and children often helped the garrison in a castle under siege by throwing rocks and hot oil on the enemy below.*

SIEGE WARFARE

To lay siege to a castle, attacking armies first had to cross the moat. They did this by filling it with stones and branches. Once they reached the castle walls, they were exposed to the defenders' arrows. But they had a number of weapons of their own. Protected behind wooden shields, they used battering rams against the walls and gateway, and huge slings to hurl rocks.

Worship of the warrior

Religion in the Middle Ages was very popular and an important part of life. Castle residents attended regular services.

Castles usually had a resident priest with whom the lord and his family attended a service every day. In early castles, the chapel was a simple room, perhaps at the top of a tower, but later it became much more important and was built near the Great Hall. The doorway into the chapel was often decorated with stone carvings, and inside there were stone columns with more carvings. Wall paintings and colorful stained glass windows depicted stories from the Bible.

At worship
The priest might be helped with the service by a monk from a nearby monastery.

Educated class

Priests were among the small number of people who could read and write at this time. Thus they were often responsible for writing and keeping records in the castle.

POWERFUL CHURCH

The Church was a very powerful institution in medieval Europe. It was also the biggest single landowner, with great estates and even castles under its control. It raised taxes to pay both for its buildings and for its priests. The head of the western Church was the Pope. Some popes tried to rival the power of kings and princes. They attempted this by relying on their religious powers over the people.

Religious establishment
This reconstruction shows Fountains Abbey in Yorkshire, England. It was founded in 1132 by an order of monks called Cistercians. It became one of the richest monasteries in northern Europe.

Sickbeds
Ill or aged monks were looked after in a building called an infirmary.

Quiet place
The cloister is an open square surrounded by covered walks where monks sat at private prayer or read.

In addition to churches and chapels, religious houses called monasteries were found in many regions. In them the resident monks or nuns spent their time in prayer, worked on the land, and also helped the needy.

Mealtimes
Monks eat together in a refectory building while one of them read aloud from religious books.

Crusading knights

Many knights went on religious wars, called Crusades. The aim was either to convert non-Christians forcibly or to drive them from lands regarded as sacred to Christians. The first Crusade was called for by Pope Urban II in 1095. Crusades continued on and off until 1500.

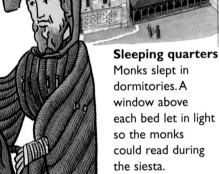

Sleeping quarters
Monks slept in dormitories. A window above each bed let in light so the monks could read during the siesta.

LEARNING CENTERS

Until universities spread through Europe in the 13th century, monasteries and abbeys were the most important centers of learning. Monks were among the few people who could read or write, and much of our knowledge of the medieval world comes from the records they kept. They also preserved books from former times by painstakingly copying out manuscripts, often illustrating, or illuminating, them beautifully.

▶ *A monk illuminates (illustrates) a book page.*

Pilgrim's progress
Many people proved their religious faith by going on arduous pilgrimages to visit shrines in places such as Rome in Italy, Santiago de Compostela in Spain, Canterbury in England, and even distant Jerusalem.

Inside a castle

Krak des Chevaliers (which means "Castle of the Knights") is the best-preserved medieval castle in the world. It dominates a high hill in Syria, and at the height of its power in about 1200, it housed a garrison of over 2,000 soldiers.

For 162 years, Krak was one of a string of castles protecting Crusader lands. During this time it survived 12 sieges and was finally taken in 1271 by Muslims after a long seige. The defenders were allowed to leave peacefully.

Turn the acetate pages *to explore medieval Krak's hidden rooms and passages. The numbers in the captions refer to both the acetates and the plan at top right.*

Krak was like a small town, with a windmill ❷, barns for storing grain ❻, and an aqueduct to supply water ❼. Two walls ❶ and ❸, and a moat ❺, provide a powerful defense. A huge sloping wall, called a talus ❹, prevented attackers from getting so close that they could not be seen by the defenders above. The castle entrance ⓫ led into a large courtyard ⓬. Meetings were held in the Great Hall ❾ under its pointed, arched roof. A Crusader chapel ❿ was built into one of the ramparts. Lookout towers ❽ jutted out from the walls.

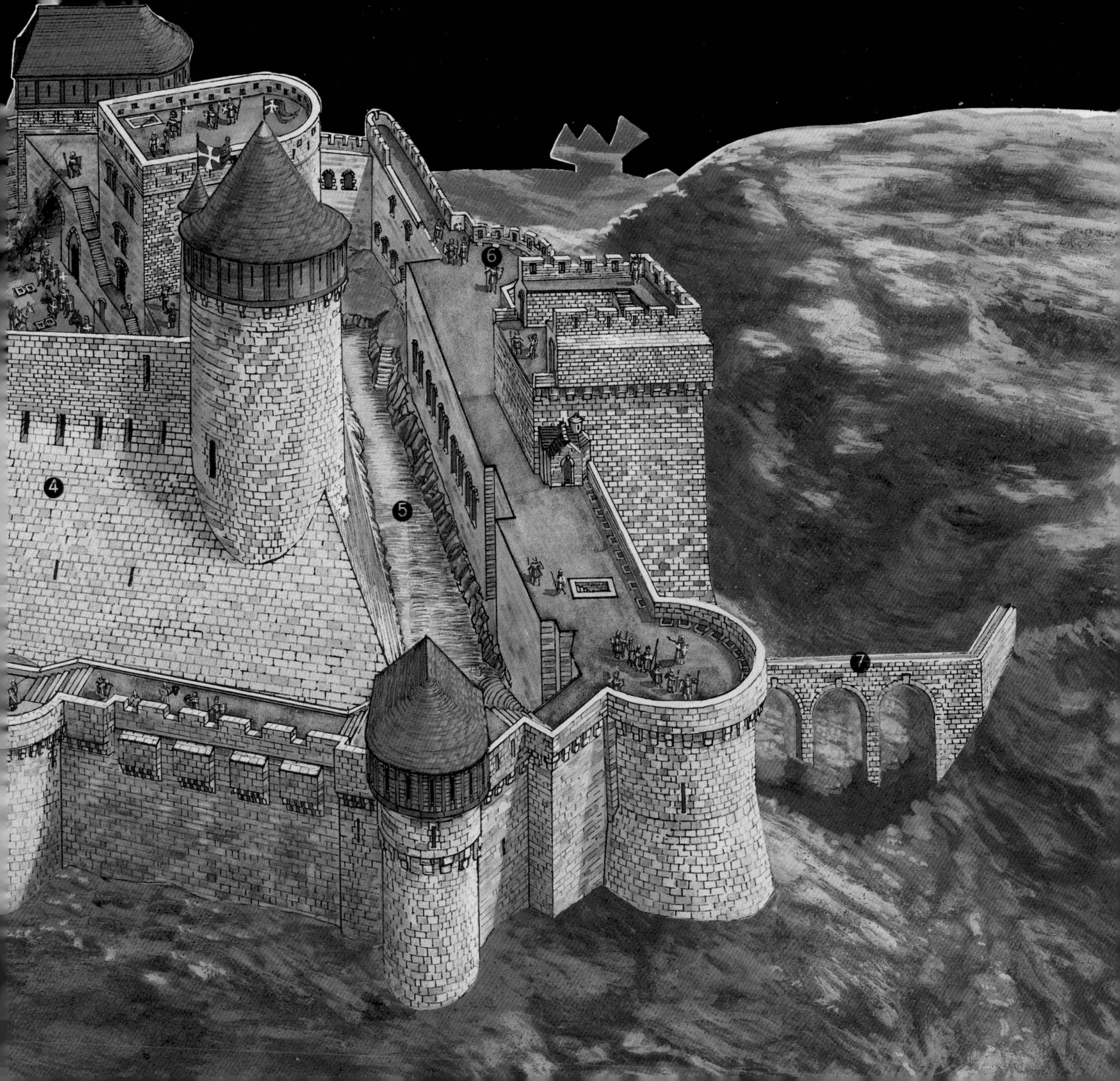
4
5
6
7

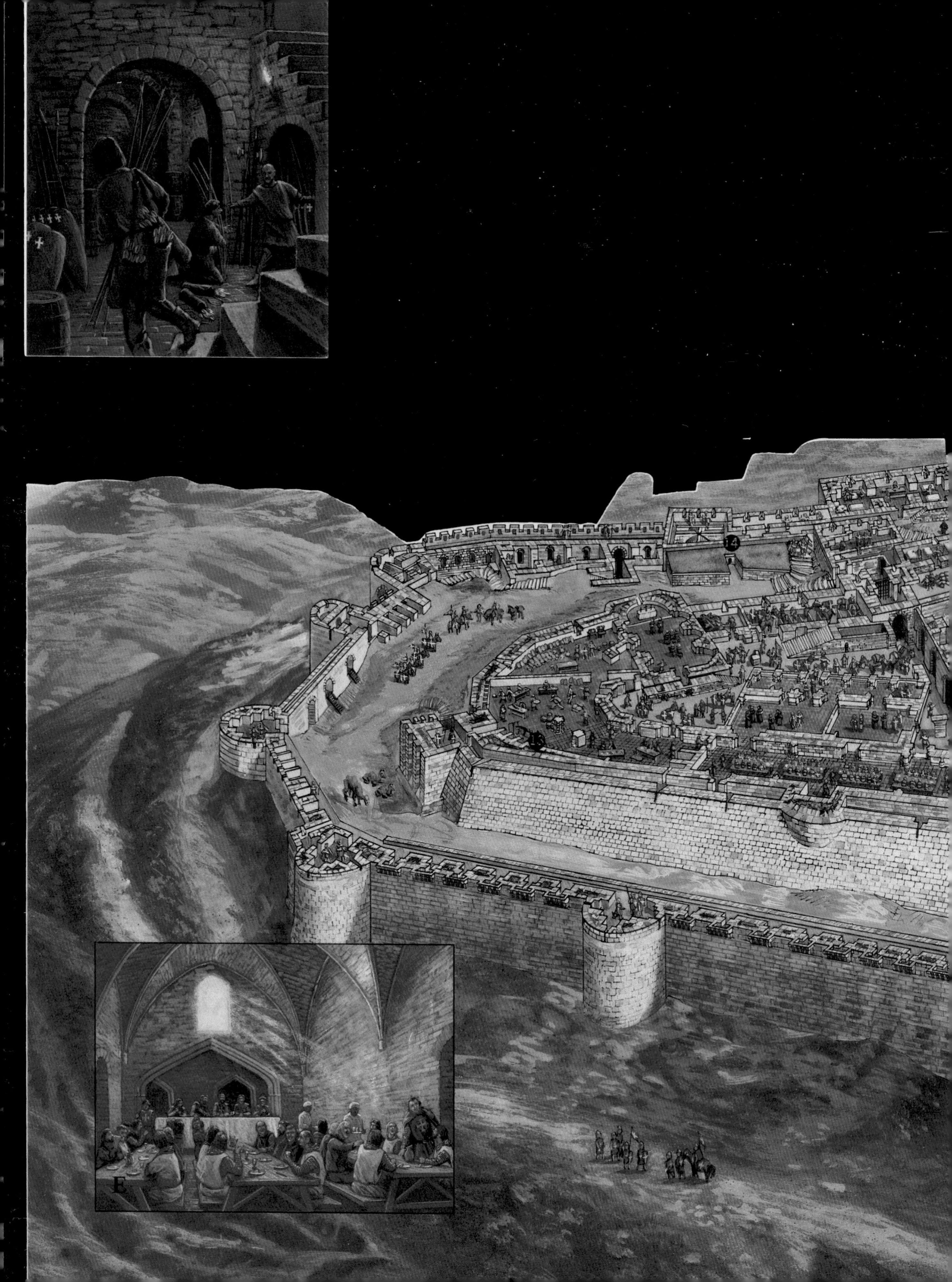
14
15
E

Plan of Krak des Chevaliers
Numbers refer to places mentioned in the text

The gigantic walls of the keep were 28 feet (8.5 m) thick at their widest points (13) *. Hidden behind the sloping wall of the talus was a long hall* (17) *which contained bread ovens and a well. Toilets were built into the far end* (18)*. Under the courtyard was the "Hall of Massive Pillars,"* (15) *which housed kitchens, dining rooms, and storerooms. The entrance passage had a sudden bend in it* (16) *to slow down any attackers who managed to get past the portcullis that protected the entrance* (14)*.*

Inset A *Krak has changed little since the Middle Ages.*
Inset B *The entrance into the castle was lined with guard rooms for extra protection.*
Inset C *Krak was controlled by a religious order of crusading.knights called Hospitalers (see page 29). Their uniform, which covered their armor, consisted of red tunics decorated with white crosses.*
Inset D *The castle storerooms held weapons and food to last at least five years.*
Inset E *Hospitalers assemble in the Great Hall.*
Inset F *Krak was captured just once, but not by force. In 1271, Sultan Baibars of Egypt tricked the Crusaders by sending them a forged letter from the Christian ruler of the area which contained orders for them to surrender.*

What was a knight?

A knight was a well-armed mounted soldier. Becoming one took bravery and devotion – knights were keen to fight in wars to prove themselves.

▲ *The squires looked after their knights. They helped them dress and cared for their weapons and horses.*

The first knights appeared in Europe in the eighth century when a new invention, the stirrup, arrived from the Orient. This device was a foot support which allowed soldiers to remain in the saddle while charging down their enemy and hitting them with force. It changed the whole nature of warfare, and as a result, medieval knights became the most important soldiers in an army. With their armor, they were the equivalent of tanks today.

As kings relied on their nobles' support to rule their lands, so the lords expected their knights to be loyal to them and support them in battle. Knights were rewarded with land or money.

◀ *A knight dressed for battle with a sword, shield, helmet, and coat of mail. His shield and banner carry his coat of arms. His squire leads his horse, which is also dressed in the knight's coat of arms.*

The price of knighthood

Knights were not as rich and powerful as the nobles, but even so,

▶ *While training for combat, squires engaged in mock jousts, using wheeled trolleys instead of horses.*

only the wealthy could afford to be knights. They wore expensive armor and rode large, expensive horses, and they needed squires and servants who had to be housed.

Some poor knights did exist, however. If a family fell on hard times, the knight might become a mercenary (a soldier paid to fight for a foreign country) or join a nobleman's retinue (paid staff). Because knights were so expensive to arm, only great lords or the king himself were rich enough to employ them.

WARRIOR MONKS

In the 12th century, during the Crusades, a group of knights was formed to protect Christian pilgrims in the Holy Land. They took monastic vows and became known as the Knights Templar, after their headquarters near the Temple in Jerusalem. At about the same time, other monks who had been looking after the sick were formed into a fighting order known as the Knights Hospitaler. These warrior monks were unquestionably brave in battle and were the mainstays of the Crusader armies.

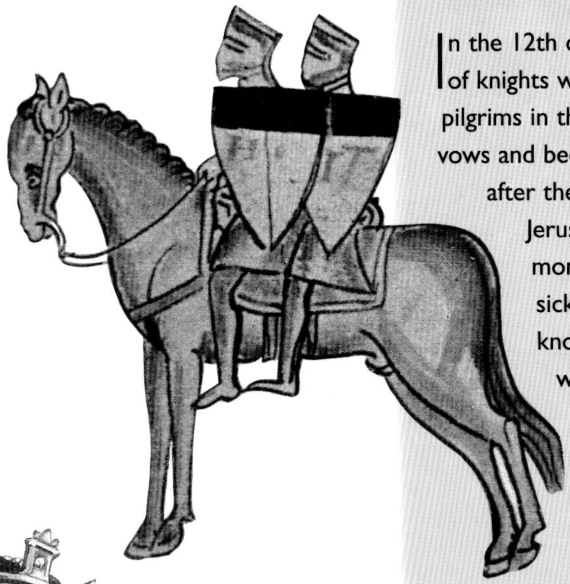

◀ *The seal of the Knights Templar showed two knights mounted on the same horse to indicate their original poverty.*

BECOMING A KNIGHT

To be a knight, a person had to be of noble birth, or come from a wealthy family. At age seven, potential knights became pages. Pages served in the castle of a great lord and took lessons in etiquette, riding, and fighting. At 14 they became squires and looked after a knight's armor, weapons, and horses. If a squire was brave in battle, he was knighted by a knight, a castle lord, or even, as in this scene, a king.

Squire being made a knight

Being knighted
With a light tap on the shoulders from a sword, a lord or other dignitary makes a squire into a knight. He is then presented with his sword and spurs.

Chivalry and heraldry

▼ This 15th-century parade shield shows a knight kneeling before his lady while death lurks in the background. The scroll above reads "You or death." A knight often carried a "favor," such as a knot of ribbons, given to him by a lady who regarded him well.

A knight's coat of arms was an important badge of honor and signified his strict codes of conduct.

To recognize who was who in battle, barons and their knights started to wear badges, called coats of arms, on their shields, on the tunics covering their armor, and on their banners and flags. Heralds, who carried messages from kings and barons to their knights and soldiers on the battlefield, had to make sure that each design was unique. They recorded the designs in books called "armorials." The system used in badge design came to be known as heraldry.

A coat of arms not only showed that a knight came from an important family, it was also a badge of honor that

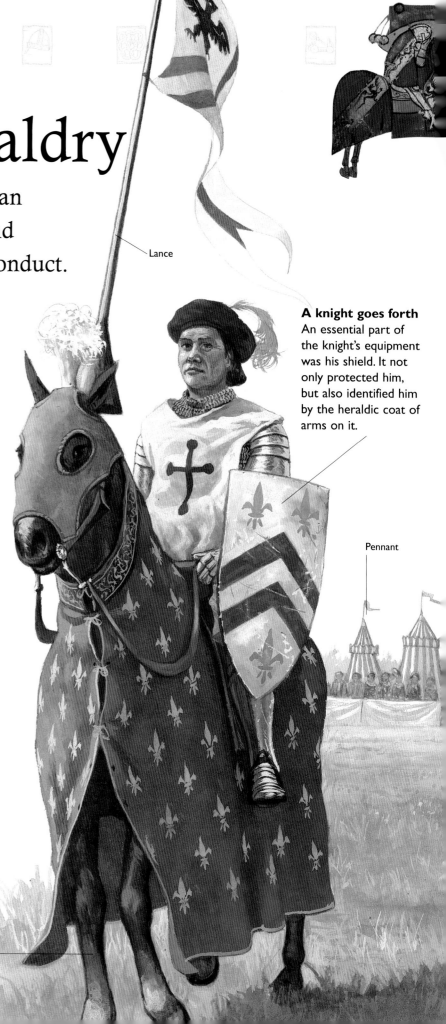

A knight goes forth
An essential part of the knight's equipment was his shield. It not only protected him, but also identified him by the heraldic coat of arms on it.

Fighting prowess
A knight's reputation depended on his fighting ability. Horsemanship was especially valued, and knights spent much time in the saddle.

◀ *Chivalry emphasized bravery, and knights were supposed to be fearless in combat. They were also – according to the ideal – to be pious, pure of heart, loyal, and generous. Chivalry also had rules governing the compassionate treatment of defeated enemies.*

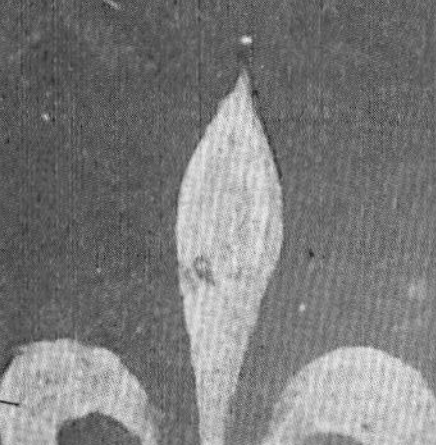

Fleur de lys

symbolized his knightly values and codes of behavior.

The codes of chivalry

From about 1150, one of the most important of these codes of conduct was "chivalry," named after the French word *chevalier* (knight). At first it meant just the skilled horsemanship of an armored warrior, but it soon became a way of life based on "fair play" and Christian values. Chivalry stressed bravery, protecting the weak, and, especially, gracious manners toward women, who were admired from afar.

Chivalric stories

Songs, poems, and tales of chivalry were written echoing this way of life. Entertainers called troubadours traveled from castle to castle singing of knightly valor and good deeds. But chivalry was an ideal which few knights lived up to. In fact, many of them were cruel and bloodthirsty.

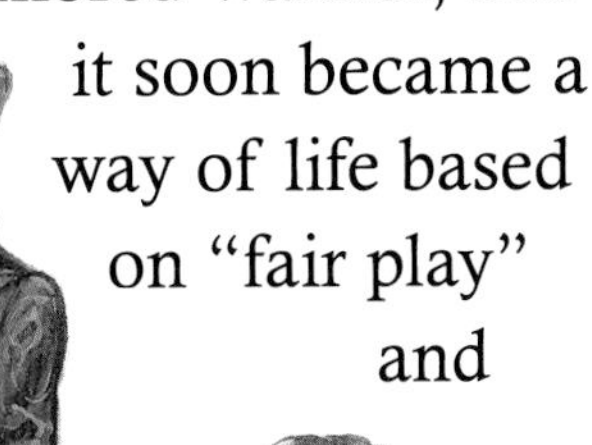

Chaste love
A knight "proved" his love for a lady by valiant deeds in combat.

Helmet

Young squire
Knights were attended by youths known as squires. As well as bearing the knights' armor, squires learned the arts of combat.

READING THE SHIELD

Some identifying designs on shields, such as the golden fleur-de-lys (the badge of royal France), were simple. Others were more elaborate. Designs on coats of arms used animals, birds, flowers, castles, and weapons. The coats of arms here are from a list made in medieval times of King Edward III of England's entourage (attendants).

Peacetime rivalry

JOUSTING FAME

Blunt-tipped lances were used during jousting, and special armor gave protection. Despite this, knights were occasionally killed during jousting. There were no rich prizes; the winner was offered the loser's horse and armor. He could either keep them or sell them back to the loser. Some poorer knights made a living going from joust to joust, winning fame and fortune through their skills.

During peacetime, knights and nobles had to stay ready for battle. War games and hunting kept them trained and fit.

Hundreds of soldiers might take part in impressive mock battles called tournaments. These huge events were held over wide areas of the countryside below the castle walls. They were spectacular occasions. The knights' costumes were emblazoned with their coats-of-arms, and they were attended by their squires and banner-bearers.

Deadly game

Early tournaments were fought like real battles, and many of the participants would be wounded,

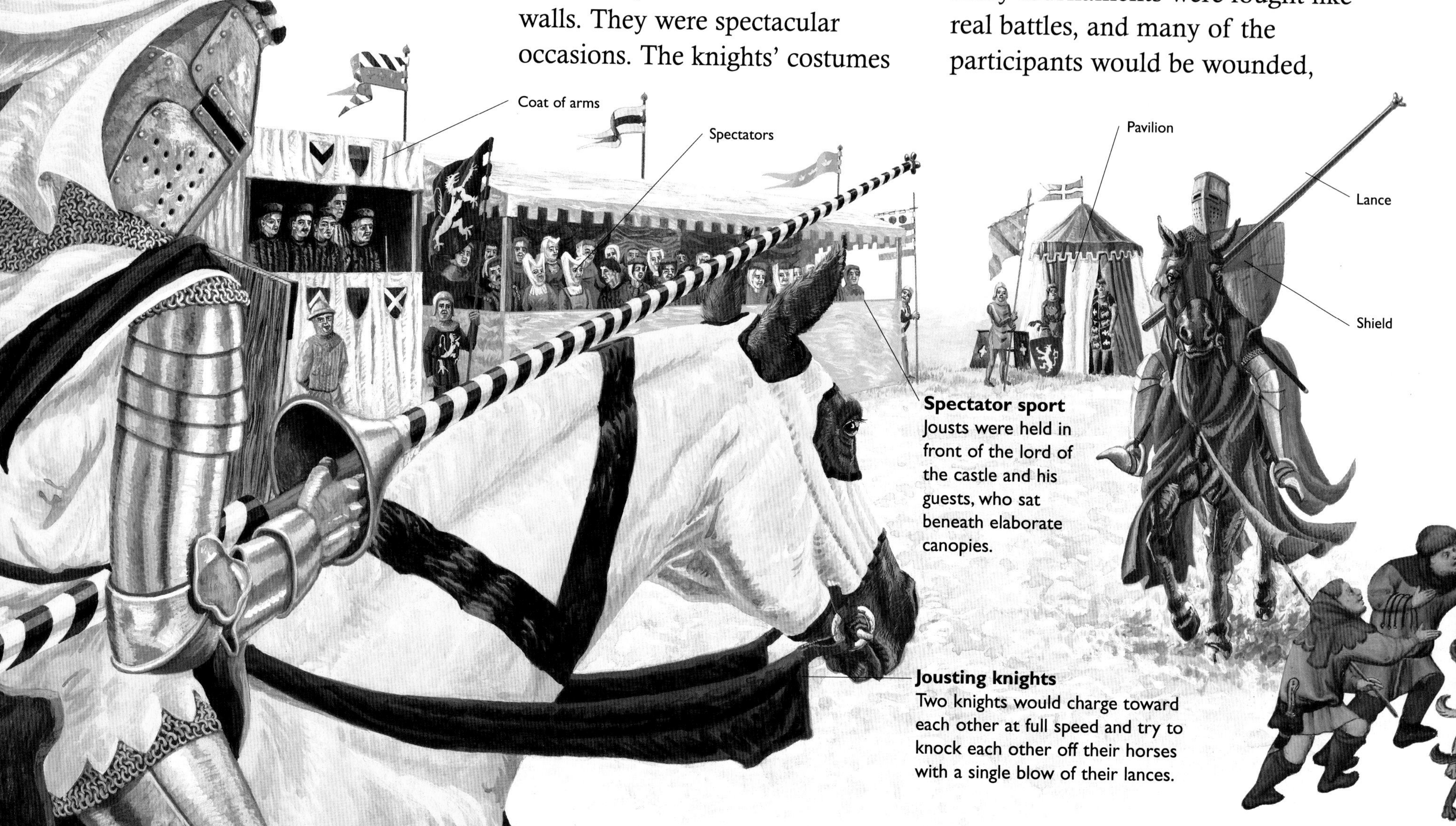

Spectator sport
Jousts were held in front of the lord of the castle and his guests, who sat beneath elaborate canopies.

Jousting knights
Two knights would charge toward each other at full speed and try to knock each other off their horses with a single blow of their lances.

◀ *The heraldic design (coat of arms) on this shield shows a covered axe. Coats of arms identified combatants in tournaments.*

▲ *Grievances between knights and nobles were often settled by a duel fought in the presence of the king. In this duel, an English squire has been accused of treason by a Frenchman.*

some even killed. Real weapons were used at first, but these were later replaced by special blunt tournament weapons. Later in the medieval period, the joust was introduced to the tournament.

Sports and pastimes

Other equally violent and competitive games were played by commoners. One of these, called bandyball, was an early form of hockey. But the most popular sport of all among the nobility was hunting.

ON THE HUNT

Horses and hounds were used to hunt wild animals such as boar, deer, wolves, and bears. But the most highly prized of all the hunting animals were birds of prey. These birds were used in the sport of falconry to catch smaller birds. Birds from the size of eagles to small hawks were used. Many of the skills and equipment were introduced from the Middle East by returning Crusaders. Falconry was, in fact, one of the most popular sports among the medieval nobility.

◀ *This hunting scene shows horsemen and hounds pursuing a stag. Hunting was considered a noble pastime, and a stag was regarded as one of the greatest prizes.*

Hounds

▲ *This 15th-century illustration shows a herb merchant selling thyme. Herbs and spices were important for flavoring and preserving food. Many came from the Orient and were so expensive that only the rich could afford them.*

In the kitchen

In the medieval castle the kitchen played a vital part. Not only did it fill the stomachs of hungry soldiers but it also turned out food fit to put on the table of the lord.

The kitchen was usually placed in a separate building in the castle courtyard. This was because of the danger of fire spreading through the rest of the castle.

In storerooms nearby, stocks of provisions were kept in preparation for a siege and in readiness for the winter when there was little fresh food available. In fact, what was cooked in the kitchen depended a great deal on the time of year and on what was being produced in the the farms and villages close to the castle. At harvest time there was plenty of food around and a wide variety, too. But in the winter the garrison survived mostly on dishes made with preserved food. The

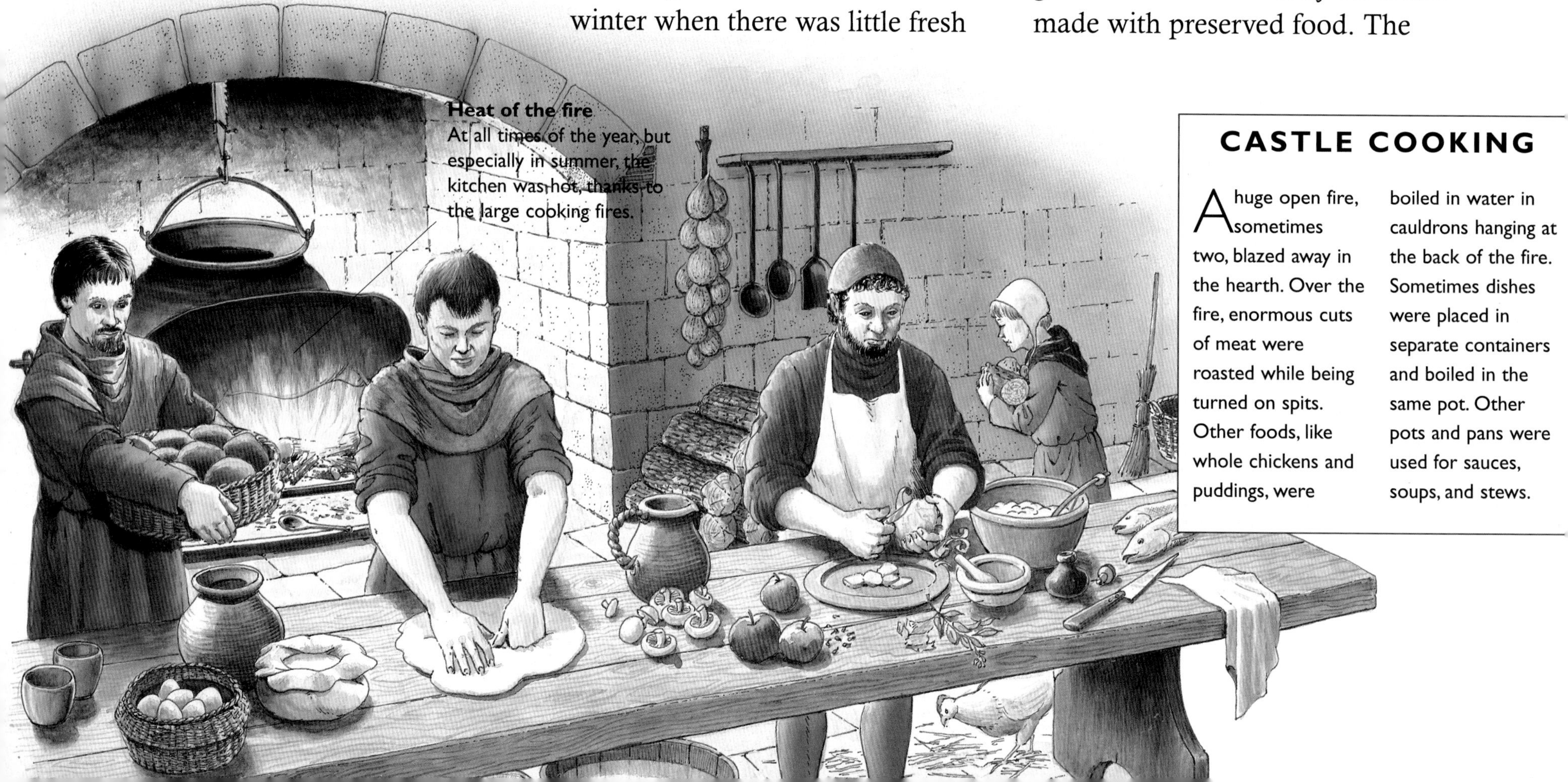

Heat of the fire
At all times of the year, but especially in summer, the kitchen was hot, thanks to the large cooking fires.

CASTLE COOKING

A huge open fire, sometimes two, blazed away in the hearth. Over the fire, enormous cuts of meat were roasted while being turned on spits. Other foods, like whole chickens and puddings, were boiled in water in cauldrons hanging at the back of the fire. Sometimes dishes were placed in separate containers and boiled in the same pot. Other pots and pans were used for sauces, soups, and stews.

food for the less exalted members of the castle community was simple fare, but if a large feast was being held in the castle, the kitchen would be in a whirl of activity. Orders were shouted by the head cook to his assistants. Meat, fish, and vegetables had to be prepared for cooking, the fire had to be stoked, water had to be fetched, and dishes, pots, and pans cleaned. Great steaming platters of food were taken to the feast, and the whole kitchen became a frantic powerhouse of heat, noise, and smell.

▲ *Despite their vital role in feeding the garrison, kitchen staff were at the bottom of the pecking order, below even the most common archer.*

▶ *Bread was the staple diet for most people in medieval times. Castle kitchens always had an oven for baking bread. Some castles even had their own windmill for making flour.*

Cooking in bulk
With a large garrison to feed, the kitchen might turn out hundreds of meals a day. Food was made in bulk, so ingredients were mixed with enormous paddles.

▼ *Cuts of meat and poultry were roasted on a spit. The grease was scooped up with giant spoons and poured over the meat to baste it.*

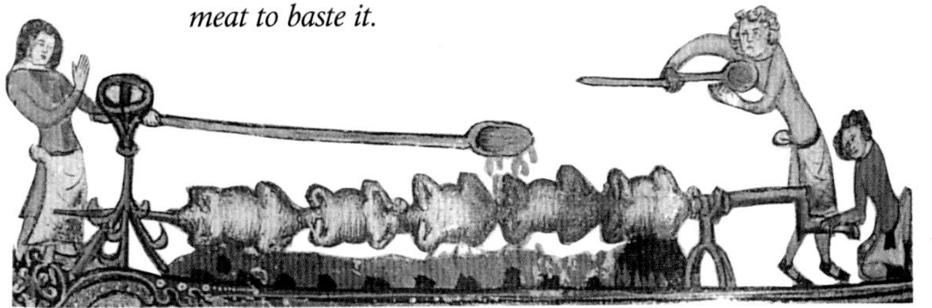

THE MEAT EATERS

Meat, including lamb, beef, and pork, made up a large part of the castle diet. Meat was preserved in salt in the fall so it would last through the winter months since it was difficult to keep livestock alive beyond the end of fall. It would be dried, salted, or smoked. But sometimes castles had their own fishponds and dovecotes(where doves are kept) to provide fresh meat throughout the year. As the meat and fish were being prepared and cooked, rich stews, soups, and sauces were cooked in cauldrons and stirred with huge sticks.

Ready for the pot
Ducks and rabbits were just some of the animals cooked in the kitchen. These two are waiting to be put in the pot.

A castle feast

Banquets or feasts were splendid occasions. They were held in the Great Hall of the castle, where all the important events took place.

The ceremony that surrounded a really grand feast was elaborate and impressive. The dishes were brought into the hall in a long procession to a fanfare of trumpets and accompanied by the chief carver and cupbearer. The lord of the castle and his lady, along with their most distinguished guests, sat at the High Table. This table was slightly raised above the others and placed at one end of the hall so that the lord could survey all his guests and they could look up to him.

At the High Table

The table for the lord was covered with a fine linen tablecloth, and the guests sat in high-backed chairs. The other guests at the feast sat on benches at lower tables ranged down the length of the hall.

◀ *A lord and his wife dine at the High Table, which is covered with a fine linen cloth. Before them a female minstrel plays a harp and sings songs.*

High Table guests might be served by pages, and their food was presented on individual plates, sometimes made of silver or gold. Other guests ate off thick slices of bread, called trenchers, which soaked up the juices of the food. Guests often brought their own flatware – knives and spoons. Forks were unknown at this point in history.

Entertainment was constant throughout the feast. The party was entertained by minstrels who sang songs and played various instruments, including pipes, drums, and lutes.

▲ *A king or great lord sometimes had a resident jester to amuse him and his guests. His jokes were often rude, and he sometimes criticized his master in ways that other people would not dare.*

FOOD AT THE FEAST

Beef, mutton, wild boar, venison, and even bear meat were eaten at feasts. Ducks, pheasants, geese, herons, peacocks, and swans were roasted and served in their feathers. Meats were often cooked with dried fruits, honey, and spices, and were served in rich sauces. Pies, fruit tarts, and milk puddings followed. Fantastically shaped sweetmeats of sugar, almond paste, and jelly might also be served to guests.

A merry time
Each course was made up of several dishes. Food was washed down with large amounts of ale (medieval beer) and wine.

Clean hands
Guests at the High Table had scented water poured on their hands, after which they dried them on linen napkins.

Everyday life

▲ *A nobleman warms his hands and feet in front of a blazing fire. Behind him, a servant brings another bundle of wood to burn.*

Early medieval castles were cold, drafty places with little furniture. Heat in winter came from great open fires that belched out smoke.

Most people in a castle, including the lord, slept on wooden benches or rough mattresses on the floor. But from about 1200, separate living quarters were built for the lord and his family, with more comfortable bed chambers and a living room called the solar. These rooms were fitted with glass windows, and the plastered walls were hung with rich tapestries. The floors were covered with fragrant flowers, such as lavender, herbs, and dried grasses.

Running the home

The lord's wife usually played an important part in running the large

HEATING THE HALL

In the Great Halls of early castles, fires were lit in the center of the floor. Great burning logs were supported by andirons (baskets made of iron bars). Smoke had to find its way out through holes in the roof.

Only during the 14th century did the open central hearth go out of common use. At this time, fireplaces with chimneys to carry away the smoke became a common feature of castle building design.

Around the fire
Family life was very important in the castle. The wife of the lord was expected to bear him a son to inherit his title, castle, and lands.

and complex household of the typical castle. With the help of her steward, ladies-in-waiting, and other servants, she was in charge of all everyday arrangements. When her husband was away, she looked after the castle estates. She visited the farms and organized supplies of food and materials for the castle, and supervised any repairs that were needed on the buildings.

MAKING MUSIC

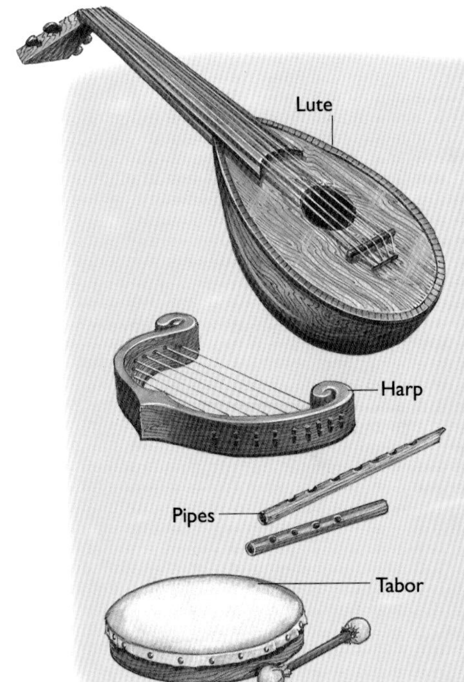

Traveling musicians called jongleurs entertained the people of the castle and were always warmly welcomed. The lords and ladies themselves liked to sing and dance, play musical instruments, and write poetry. The lute – played like a guitar – became popular in the 14th century. Small hand-held drums called tabors were common in the Middle Ages and so were flutes, pipes, harps, and wind instruments.

Home entertainment

Most castle occupants did not know how to read or write. Keeping amused, especially in the winter, was a problem. They spent the long evenings playing board games, such as chess, or listened to storytellers who recited poems of love and chivalry.

Passing time
During winter evenings, a lord and his friends might retire to his private rooms to play a game of chess.

Your move
Chess was introduced to Europe from the Middle East. It became very popular with the nobility.

Castle clothes

Medieval clothes were made by hand, one at a time. Most clothes were plain and practical – those that were made of expensive fabrics were highly prized.

▲ *The poor wore simple clothes made of thick wool and hemp (a rough fiber similar to cotton). These garments were made to last many years.*

Most people owned few clothes, and those that were good quality would be passed down from parents to their children. Sometimes a king or nobleman gave his clothes to his servants as a form of payment. Clothes had to be well-made if they were to last. The fabrics used included wool, linen, a coarse fiber called hemp, and, for the very rich, costly silks and velvets imported from Italy and the Orient. All these materials were spun and woven using hand-operated spinning wheels and looms. They were then cut and sewn, also by hand.

◀ *Clothes worn by the nobility were made of rich silks and velvets, often trimmed with fur.*

▶ *Working people's clothes had to be practical, so a smith wears a leather apron.*

A peasant

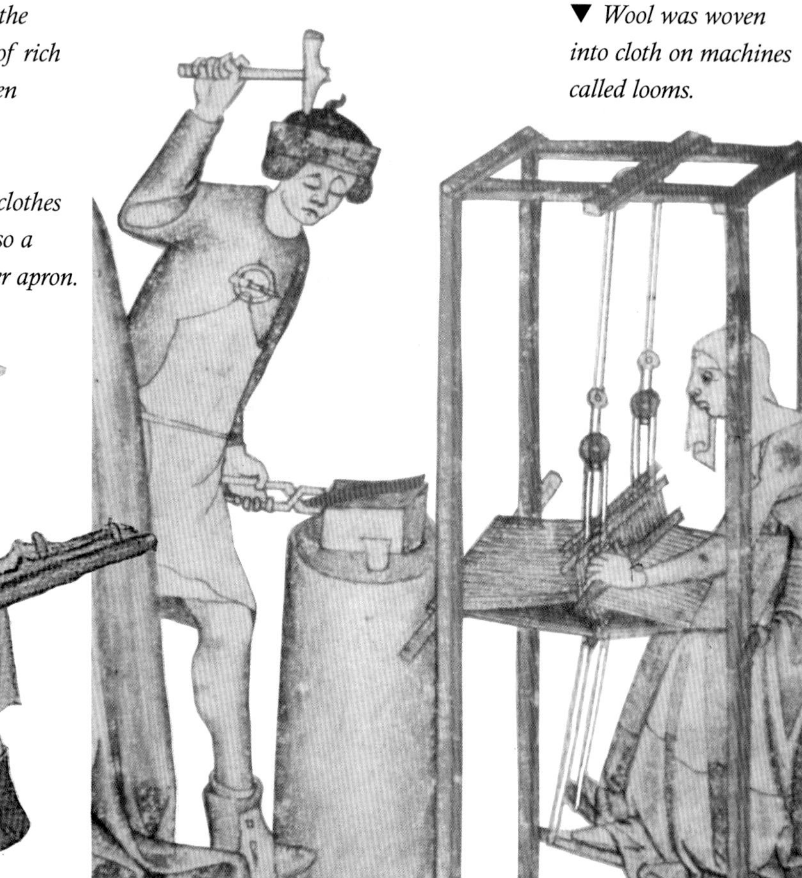

▼ *Wool was woven into cloth on machines called looms.*

LORDS OF FASHION

Just as they built their castles to impress, so lords and knights wanted to outdo each other with the richness of their clothes. This was especially true on formal occasions such as feasts or royal visits. Lords and ladies wore gold chains and beautiful jewelry. Some of the clothes became so outrageous and expensive that laws, called sumptuary laws, were introduced in many parts of Europe trying to ban them.

Styles of clothing

Early in medieval times the rich wore fairly simple clothes. But from the 12th century, fashions became much more elaborate, with brightly colored clothes, hats, shoes, and extravagant hairstyles.

At the same time, less wealthy people could not afford to take any interest in fashion. Their clothes were simple and hard-wearing, and far more practical than those of the rich. They made their own clothes and wore smocks, tunics, and thick wool stockings to keep out the cold. With regular repairs, these tough clothes lasted for years.

Being dressed
Attended by her maid and lady-in-waiting, a noblewoman is being dressed and her hair prepared.

Lady-in-waiting
A lady-in-waiting helped a member of a royal household with her official duties.

Maids' duties
Maids performed the domestic duties for an important woman.

Ladies' clothing
Over her fine linen underdress, the lady will wear a dress of rich silk or velvet, perhaps trimmed with fur.

Hair care
The lady's hair will be held up under an elaborate headdress with a flowing veil.

Bathtime
Bathing in a tub was rare even for the rich. To bathe, hot water was poured into a wooden tub lined with a cloth.

Health and hygiene

Baths were rarely taken and, with no sewage systems, castles and their inmates must have smelled. Lack of knowledge about germs meant early death was common.

Cleanliness certainly did not play a very important part in the lives of medieval people. Only the most sophisticated people wished to have even an occasional bath. Most of the time castles were breeding grounds for germs. Sewage was slopped into moats although care was taken not to pollute drinking water in the well.

Medical knowledge
People in medieval Europe had no understanding of germs and the

Getting clean
Scented oils were added to the water to clean and freshen the skin.

GARDEROBES

Toilets in castles were primitive: they were just holes in wooden seats. One or two would be placed in small rooms, known as garderobes, on the outer walls of the castle. The waste dropped down a chute either to a pit below or straight into the waters of the moat. The lord and lady sometimes had pots, in the privacy of their chamber, which were emptied by servants every morning.

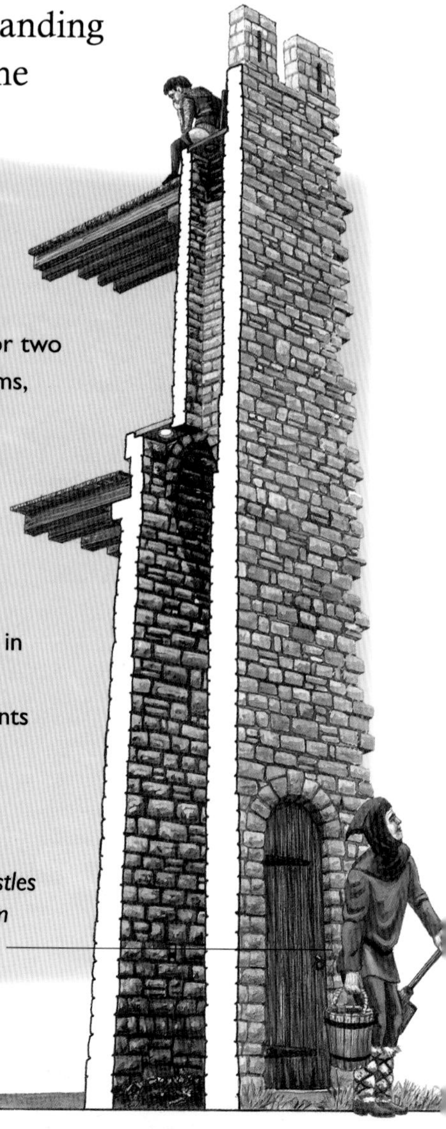

In addition to occasional removal of latrine waste, castles were cleaned and aired from top to bottom once a year.

◀ *A man is struggling with Death, who is represented by this gruesome skeleton. Death lurked everywhere in medieval times: diseases killed adults and children, rich and poor.*

ARAB WISDOM

The health, hygiene, and medical knowledge of the Arab world was far more advanced than that of medieval Europe. Returning Crusaders brought back some of this knowledge, such as the writings of Muslim doctors and scientists like Ibn Sina (known in Europe as Avicenna) and al-Razi (Rhazes). These books were studied all over Europe and did much to improve standards of medical care.

spread of disease in dirty living conditions. Lice and fleas lived in people's hair, and these insects carried disease from animals to humans and from person to person. Because of this, in just three years (1347–49) a terrible plague – the Black Death – killed more than one fourth of the people of Europe. Infections also killed many others because doctors did not understand the importance of keeping wounds clean.

▼ *Using a large pair of pliers, a "doctor" removes an arrow from a man's back. There were no effective anesthetics, and European surgical skills were very basic. Many died of blood loss or blood poisoning.*

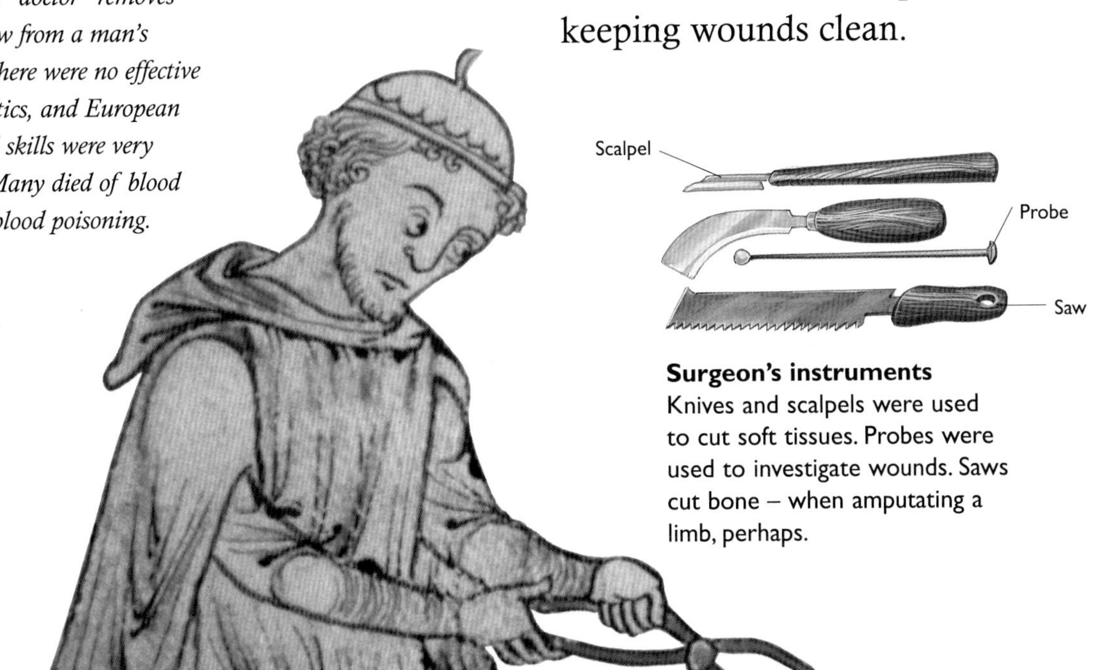

Surgeon's instruments
Knives and scalpels were used to cut soft tissues. Probes were used to investigate wounds. Saws cut bone – when amputating a limb, perhaps.

▲ *A Muslim doctor takes the pulse of a patient. Treatment of the sick and injured in medieval Europe could have very uncertain results. There was a high chance that patients would end up in a worse condition.*

Castles worldwide

Castles, fortresses, and walled towns are found all over the world, from the Americas and Europe to the Middle East, Africa, India, and Japan.

Aleppo Citadel, *Syria*
This huge fortress stands on a small hill and dominates Aleppo, one of the oldest cities in the world. It was built at the end of the 12th century after the Arab leader Saladin's successes against the Crusaders. A huge ditch surrounds the walls, and the fortress is entered by an enormous stone tower and bridge.

Caernarfon, *Wales*
The original wooden motte-and-bailey castle built on this site in 1090 was completely rebuilt in stone by King Edward I of England between 1283 and 1330. Edward is considered to be one of the great castle builders of the Middle Ages. The defensive structures at Caernarfon Castle included five doors, two drawbridges, and six portcullises!

▲ *Castel Coca in Castile, Spain, is decorated with elaborate patterns of bricks. Its walls are protected by overhanging turrets and contain gun ports. The walls that can be seen today were built on 11th- and 12th-century foundations.*

Carcassonne, *France*
Despite heavy restorations in the 19th century, Carcassonne is the best surviving example of a medieval fortified town. The fortifications were begun in 1130 and continued until the late 13th century. An inner and outer wall is interspersed with round towers all the way along.

Castel del Monte, *Italy*
The German Emperor Frederick II built this castle in about 1240. It is unusual in that it was designed more as a hunting lodge than a fortress. Its plan is also entirely symmetrical: an octagonal wall surrounds an octagonal courtyard, with octagonal towers at the corners and eight rooms on each of the two floors!

Chateau Gaillard, *France*
At the turn of the 13th century, this castle –

◀ *The "fairytale" castle of Neuschwanstein, Germany, was built by King Ludwig of Bavaria toward the end of the 19th century. At this time, many people had a romantic image of the medieval era.*

now lying in ruins – was one of the finest in France, with a massive keep surrounded by towering walls. It was built between 1196 and 1198 by King Richard I of England, who then ruled part of France.

Coca Castle, *Spain*
This late medieval Muslim castle is constructed of brick, with four octagonal towers placed around its walls. Its blending of Muslim and Western styles of achitecture – known as "Mudejar" – makes it one of Spain's most magnificent castles.

Fort Duquesne, *U.S.A.*
The French built this frontier fort in the 1750s to control vital river communications. Despite having square wooden walls that were strengthened by earth banks, it was captured by the British in 1758 and was renamed Fort Pitt. Pittsburgh grew up around it.

Gent Castle, *Belgium*
The fortresses of Syria were the inspiration for this massive castle, begun in 1180 by the Crusader knight Philip of Alsace. It was one of the strongest castles in Belgium, with a square keep and a deep moat surrounding the walls.

Great Zimbabwe, *Zimbabwe*
The fortified town of Great Zimbabwe was built between about 1000 and 1500, but is now partly ruined. Geometric patterns were included in the design of the stone walls, which today stand more than 30ft (10m) high.

Gwalior Fort, *India*
Routes into central and southern India were protected by this huge fortress-palace, built in about 1500. It stands high on a rock and has flat walls punctuated by circular towers with golden domes.

Himeji Castle, *Japan*
This elegant castle was begun in the mid-14th century and was not completed until as late as 1609. Its thick, curving walls, which once protected against rebellious warlords, now withstand the shock of earthquakes, which are frequent in Japan.

Kremlin, *Russia*
Built in Moscow in the 12th century, the Kremlin is a huge city-fortress that encloses palaces, churches, and other buildings. Its pink-colored walls stand nearly 66 feet (20m) high with 19 towers. Today it houses government offices and a world-famous museum.

Machu Picchu, *Peru*
This fortress-city, built by the Incas in around 1500, could be defended by just a few soldiers: it lies 8,000 ft (2,500 m) high up the Andes Mountains, which run down Peru, and it could be reached only by tortuous staircases.

Neuschwanstein Castle, *Germany*
This fairytale mountain castle was built by King Ludwig II of Bavaria (the name for a region of Germany) between 1869 and 1881. It is a fantastic creation with elaborately designed towers and turrets that reflected King Ludwig's romantic view of medieval life and architecture. It served no defensive purpose whatsoever.

Red Fort, *India*
The Indian Emperor Akbar the Great built the Red Fort between 1564 and 1580 on the foundations of an earlier castle. It stands beside the River Jumna at Agra, and its huge red sandstone outer wall is over 1 mile (1.6 km long).

Tower of London, *England*
William the Conqueror, King of England between 1066 and 1087, built this royal palace fortress in about 1080. A huge keep called the White Tower stands at its center. The White Tower was later used as a prison where some of the most important people in England were kept.

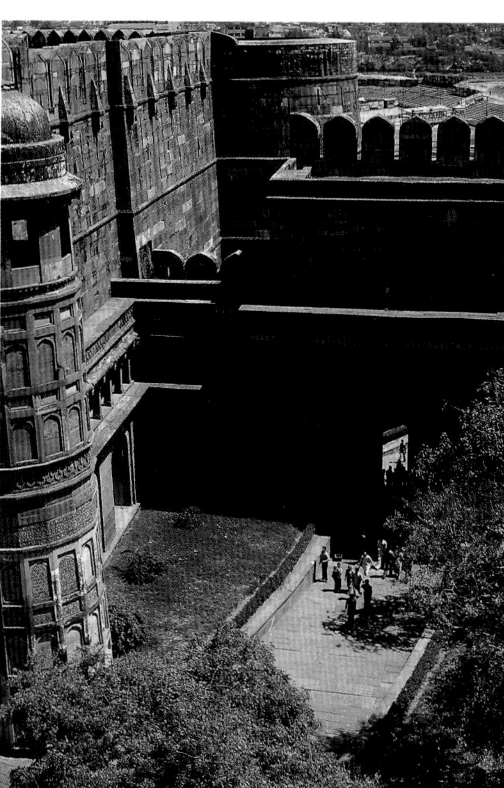

▲ *The Red Fort at Agra, India, was rebuilt by Akbar (1542–1605), the greatest of the line of emperors known as the Moguls. Inside its massive red sandstone walls are a palace and two mosques.*

Index

Page numbers in *italic* refer to illustrations

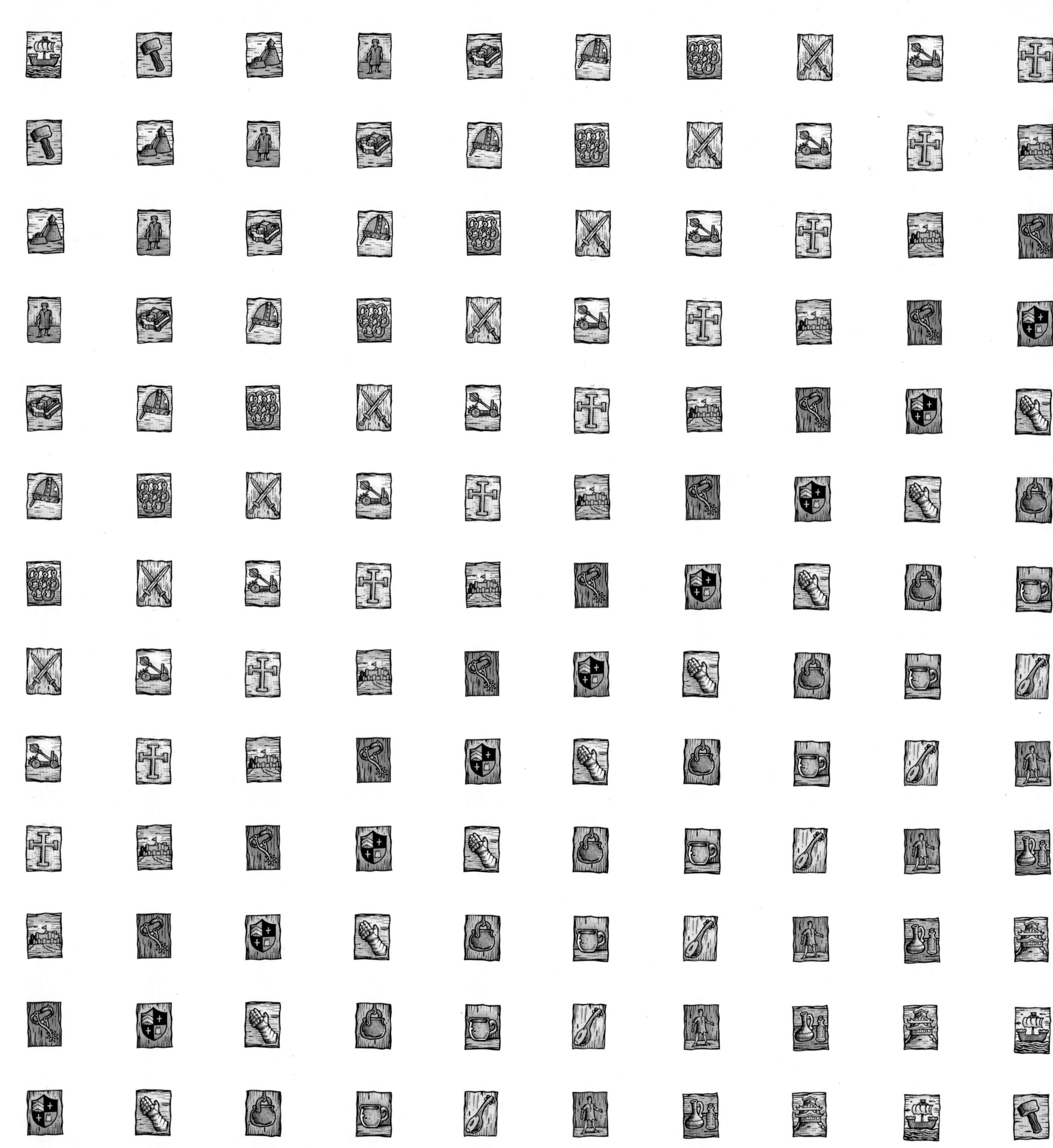